P9-CFJ-817

LINCOLN CHRISTIAN COLLEGE AND SEMINARY

Women & Men

Gender in the Church

page 2 blank

Women  Men
Gender in the Church

Edited by **Carol Penner**

Sponsored by Women's Concerns Committees, Mennonite Central Committee U.S. and Mennonite Central Committee Canada

Mennonite
Publishing
House

Waterloo, Ontario
Scottdale, Pennsylvania

Canadian Cataloguing-in-Publication Data
Women and men : gender in the church
"Sponsored by Women's Concerns Committees, Mennonite Central
Committee U.S. and Mennonite Central Committee Canada."
Includes bibliographical references.
ISBN 0-8361-9079-3
1. Sex role—Religious aspects—Christianity. I. Penner, Carol, 1960-
BT708.W65 1998   261.8'343   C98-931371-9

The paper used in this publication is recycled and meets the minimum require-
ments of the American National Standard for Information Sciences—
Permanence of Paper for Printed Library Materials. ANSI Z39.48-1984.

Unless otherwise noted, Scripture is from *The New Revised Standard Version
Bible*, Copyright 1989 by the Division of Christian Education of the National
Council of the Churches of Christ in the USA, and is used by permission.
Phillips, from *The New Testament in Modern English,* Macmillan Publishing
Company.

WOMEN AND MEN: GENDER IN THE CHURCH
Copyright ©1998 by Herald Press, Waterloo, Ont. N2L 6H7
Published simultaneously in USA by Herald Press,
Scottdale, Pa. 15683. All rights reserved
Library of Congress Catalog Card Number: 98-72959
Canadiana Entry Number: C98-931371-9
International Standard Book Number: 0-8361-9079-3
Printed in the United States of America
Book and cover design by Paula M. Johnson

07 06 05 04 03 02 01 00 99 98 10 9 8 7 6 5 4 3 2 1

Contents

96622

Foreword

THE WOMEN'S CONCERNS Committees (Canada and U.S.) of Mennonite Central Committee have had a long-standing commitment to work on issues of abuse in the church and in Christian families.

We have produced packets of helpful material: "Broken Boundaries," on child sexual abuse; "Crossing the Boundaries," on pastoral and professional sexual abuse; and a "Purple Packet," on spouse abuse.

More recently, we've published a booklet that addresses the needs of family members of both the survivors and the perpetrators of sexual abuse: *Expanding the Circle of Caring.* Another booklet of worship resources assists congregations in breaking the silence surrounding abuse: *Lord, Hear Our Prayers.**

All these resources briefly deal with abuse prevention. But their primary focus is on what to do after abuse has occurred. Recently we at MCC Women's Concerns evaluated our work on issues of abuse.

In the context of that evaluation, we heard a strong call to explore ways in which our beliefs about God and our

---

* These packets and booklets are available from Women's Concerns: MCC Canada, 134 Plaza Dr., Winnipeg, MB R3T 5K9; or MCC U.S., P.O. Box 500, Akron, PA 17501-0500.

assumptions about our roles as men and women may contribute to abuse. We were asked to work on our theology and thinking about gender. These fundamental beliefs shape how women and men treat each other.

We have looked for ways to address concretely a theology of gender, a topic which at first seemed rather abstract. One of the most powerful tools we have found is a simple exercise used in the context of MCC orientation sessions on gender.

In those sessions, we ask all women present to sit in a small inner circle and ask the men to sit in an outer ring around the women's circle. While the men listen in silence, the women talk about one question: "What is God calling me to as a woman?"

Then after about twenty minutes, the men and women switch places. The women listen as the inner circle of men apply the question to themselves: "What is God calling me to as a man?"

Finally, we ask both groups to discuss what they observed about the differences between the two groups, differences in both conversational style and content.

What emerges is unpredictable but always illuminating for all of us. People on the outside circle usually listen with the curiosity of eavesdroppers. Those on the inside generally forget about the outer circle and speak freely, as if they are enjoying an opportunity that people seldom have.

One man commented that as he listened, he felt he was on holy ground. Such occasions of listening in while some of the opposite sex speak freely do not occur naturally. They need to be created and protected. It is our hope that this book will provide a catalyst for such conversations.

This study book is not intended to offer final answers. Instead, it is meant to provide a forum for discussion and a stimulus for new thinking.

The chapters are designed to generate conversation in ways that help women and men explore their own experiences and arrive at their own solutions. If we truly listen and share with respect for all, we will learn from each other and grow in applying our faith to daily life.

We are grateful for the excellent work that Carol Penner has done in shaping this book, finding authors for the various chapters, and editing the parts to make a coherent whole. The subject of gender can at times feel too abstract to discuss. Through the stories Carol has collected, she has made gender issues personal and understandable.

All of us are indebted to the authors for writing from their areas of expertise and for exploring their own personal experience with candor and insight.

We at the MCC U.S. and MCC Canada Women's Concerns desks truly hope that this volume will be used as a tool in Christian education classes, for small-group studies, and for personal reflection.

—*Gwen M. Groff*
Director of MCC U.S. Women's Concerns
Akron, Pennsylvania

—*Eleanor Epp-Stobbe*
MCC Canada Women's Concerns Coordinator
Winnipeg, Manitoba

Editor's Preface

Why do we need a book about gender in the church?

BEING WOMEN AND BEING MEN, we share a lot in common. We all live on the same earth, we breathe the same air, and we've been created by the same God. We share similar needs—food, water, warmth, clothing, shelter, and love. When we unite in prayer, we know that God hears each of us. Why do we need to talk about gender in the church at all?

I can answer that with a question: When we see a baby, why is it important to know whether it's a boy or a girl? Why are we uneasy when we don't know if an androgynous-looking adult is male or female? The social structures we live in have different messages for male and female bodies. We are raised to live in the world as gendered people.

Because gender is so integral to who we are, it's a part of our faith. Being men and being women, we have different experiences. In the context of these experiences, we encounter God. This book has been sponsored by MCC (Mennonite Central Committee) Women's Concerns to encourage dialogue around the issues where gender and faith meet.

You will likely not agree with everything you read in this book! Many writers have worked together to produce this study, and they have varied points of view. What they share in common is an understanding that gender shapes our faith, and that as women and men we need to learn from each other. My experience has been that people have strong opinions about issues surrounding gender. In your discussions, you likely will see that, too.

You may not feel comfortable talking about some subjects raised heres. Our bodies have usually not been something we discuss, particularly in the church. If you are studying this books with others, I invite you to be sensitive to the dynamics in your group. In responding to questions, are women's and men's voices given equal hearing? If your group is large you may want to divide for some discussions, so women and men can process a topic separately. Then you can come back together to share perspectives.

The only way to learn from each other is to listen to each other. I hope this book will encourage you to listen and explore what it means to be women and men together in the church.

Thanks to Tina Mast Burnett, Eleanor Epp-Stobbe, and Kathy Shantz for their wisdom and patience in seeing this book through the writing and editing stages.

I also give thanks to the following people for their helpful insight and for their work in reading a draft of this book.

Martha Smith Good
Anne Findlay-Chamberlain
Marlene Kroeker
Marlene Kropf
Ingrid Janzen Lamp
David Schroeder

—*Carol Penner, Editor*
Vineland, Ontario

1

Gender in the Old Testament

Wilma Ann Bailey

Wilma Ann Bailey is associate professor of biblical studies and religion at Messiah College. She serves on the Mennonite Central Committee U.S. Board and has served on the Mennonite Board of Education. She has written and spoken on women in the Old Testament, dignity, and a variety of other topics.

STUDYING GENDER issues in ancient Israel through the lens of the biblical text is a lot like studying gender issues in the United States solely by watching professional football games. Football, for the most part, is a man's game. Men organize it, compete in it, watch it, and analyze it. Women appear at halftime to entertain, cheer the players on, and replenish the snacks. But one would develop a distorted view of the roles of men and women in late-twentieth-century America if one's study were limited to professional football!

Much (but by no means all) of the materials in the Old

Testament are written from the perspective of men and focus on the world of men (priests, kings, warriors, clan leaders, and so on), particularly in the legal and narrative texts. Because of this perspective, relationships between the sexes and the role of women in ancient Israel are obscured.

Anthropologists have learned through research that there are no universal roles for women or men beyond those of biological necessity (with the possible exception of clearing virgin forest land, which so far has universally proved to be a job for men). Women nurse infants, but the one who cares for children beyond infancy varies depending on the culture. Food preparation is often a woman's job, but in some traditional Pacific-island societies, men do the cooking.

In the United States until recent decades, the vast majority of medical doctors were men, and medicine was considered to be a profession best suited to men. In the former Soviet Union, the vast majority of medical doctors were women, and medicine was considered to be a profession best suited to women.

We know little about the realities of everyday life on the level of gender in ancient Israel, and we must be careful not to impose our own socially conditioned notions of gender roles onto that society.

Patriarchy and Matriarchy

The dominant text of the Old Testament reflects a patriarchal and patrilineal social organization for ancient Israel. This means that men generally held leadership positions, and the line of descent was traced from father to son.

There is, however, evidence of an earlier matriarchy. For example, in Genesis the man is to leave his parents and go to his wife (2:24). An excited Rebekah runs to inform her "mother's house" of a stranger in town (Gen. 24:28; see also Ruth 1:8). Rival co-wives Leah and Rachel name their children (Gen. 30). And with Abraham and Sarah, there is a marriage of brother and half sister (Gen. 20:12; see also 2 Sam. 13:13).

All of these reflect either matrilocal, matrilineal, or matriarchal social organization. Scholar André LaCocque believes that the ancient Near East was matriarchal prior to an Indo-European invasion of about 2500 B.C., bringing patriarchal structures of social organization.

Male-Female Equality

In the opening chapter of the Old Testament, the intrinsic equality of males and females is affirmed. Both are created in the divine image. Both are given authority over animal life. Both are commanded to be fruitful and multiply, filling the earth and caring for it. This opening chapter of Genesis represents the mature fruit of Israelite theology on the issue of gender.

The Hebrew Bible (our Old Testament) understands inequality and hierarchy in male and female roles and status to be a result and reflection of sin (Gen. 3). LaCocque writes, "The rule of man over woman is a sign of the perversion of creation by the human couple . . ." (13; see list below). It is ironic that the Christian community has chosen to use as its model the perverted relationship between the sexes found in Genesis 3 rather than the ideal relationship based on equality. God commanded and intended equality, according to Genesis 1.

Gender in the Legal Texts

The scholar Phyllis Bird points out that the (Hebrew) language of the legal texts usually indicates that men are the audience. Exodus 20:17 says, "You shall not covet your neighbor's wife." Much of casuistic law (case law) is cast in the form, "If a man [Hebrew: *ish*, a male; not the generic *adam*, human being] does such and such, then so and so will be the result" (see Exod. 21:12). Sometimes the language is clearly inclusive, as in Exodus 21:28: "When an ox gores a man or a woman. . . ."

Since much of the law directs public life, the language may be cast in masculine form because men were more likely to be involved in public activities. We expect that women involved in public activities would be subject to the same laws.

In biblical law, there is equality of punishment but not equality of definition. In the case of adultery, men and women receive the same punishment—death (Lev. 20:10). But the definition of what constitutes adultery for men and women is not the same.

A woman is expected to engage in intimate relations solely with her husband, or she is an adulteress. A man may engage in intimate relations with other women and not be an adulterer unless the other woman is married (Gen. 38:12-24; 1 Sam. 1:2). A man may put his wife through an ordeal if he suspects her of being unfaithful, but there is no comparable ordeal for a man suspected of being unfaithful (Num. 5:11-31).

On the other hand, according to the law, mothers are to be honored along with fathers (Exod. 20:12).

In the book of Numbers (chap. 27), the daughters of a man named Zelophehad petition Moses to permit them to inherit their father's estate because he left no sons. Moses brings the request before God, who supports the request of the women.

Furthermore, God commands that it will be a permanent law in Israel that women may inherit the family estate if there are no sons. This contrasts sharply with the usual practice in patriarchal societies: in the absence of a son, the estate passes to the closest male relative.

The fifth book of the law, Deuteronomy (chap. 22), contains a series of laws regulating sexual activity. In 22:23-29, the question is whether or not intercourse between two people not married to each other was consensual, with both agreeing. There are different rules, depending on the setting.

If a man engages in intercourse with an engaged woman in town, both are to be stoned, but for different reasons: the man because he violated "his neighbor's wife," and the woman because she did not cry out for help. The assumption is that if she were being raped, she would have screamed. And in a town, someone would have heard her and come to her rescue or at least borne witness that the intercourse was not consensual.

However, if the intercourse took place in the country-side, there were no witnesses to verify whether or not she had consented. If the woman says she was raped, the man is to be executed. The man is to be executed solely on the word of the woman! The assumption is that if a woman says she was raped, she most likely was, and she is to be believed.

Gender in the Narrative Texts, Wisdom Literature, and Prophecy

As Phyllis Bird points out, women appear in the narrative texts of the Old Testament primarily as wives, mothers (Gen. 30), daughters (Judg. 11:34-40; 2 Kings 11:2-3), and sisters (Exod. 2:4; Gen. 34:13-31). They also are found as judges (Judg. 4-5), midwives (Exod. 1:15), prophets (2 Kings 22; Judg. 4:4; Exod. 15:20), worship leaders (Exod. 15:20-21), civic leaders (2 Sam. 20:16-22; Mic. 6:4), warriors (Judg. 5:24-27), businesswomen (Prov. 31:18, 24), and reigning monarchs (2 Kings 11). Perhaps some of the queens were actually co-regents. Jezebel, for example, seems to wield quite a bit of power.

The narrative texts include stories about men who love their wives and are devoted to them (1 Sam. 1:5; Gen. 29:18), and about women who love and are devoted to their husbands (1 Sam. 18:20; 19:11-17). Yet marriages were usually arranged based upon economic and family considerations in the ancient Near East.

The narratives texts also contain stories depicting horrendous acts of physical and emotional abuse of women (Gen. 34:2; Judg. 19:25-29; 2 Sam. 13:11-14). Such episodes no doubt mirror occurrences in the everyday life of the ancient Israelite community (see Trible, *Texts of Terror*). Tales of women who use their sexuality to entrap men have also found their way into the biblical narrative (Judg. 16:4-21).

Several stories in the Old Testament center around the theme of men being rescued by women. Rahab, a woman living in the city of Jericho, protects the Israelite spies from her townsmen (Josh. 2). Rebekah rescues Jacob from his brother's wrath (Gen. 27:42-43). Sarah risks sexual compromise to prevent Abraham from being harmed (Gen. 12:11-13). Jael shatters the skull of Sisera, commander of the enemy army, hastening the end of the war with the Hazorites (Judg. 4:17-22; 5:24-27).

In the time of the kings, Michal saves David from certain death at the hands of her father, Saul (2 Sam. 19:11-17). The woman of Abel-Beth-Maacah protects her city from the Israelite army (2 Sam. 20:14-22).

An interesting text in Deuteronomy assumes that there will be situations when two men are fighting and a woman must step in to rescue her husband (Deut. 25:11). The woman as the protector of men is a biblical theme that has been little explored.

Female imagery is used in Wisdom literature and in Lamentations, among other places. Wisdom is personified as a woman in the book of Proverbs (chap. 4), as is folly (chap. 5). The figures of the widow and the raped virgin depict the sorrowful state of Jerusalem following its conquest by the Babylonian army (Lam. 1; 5:11).

The prophetic literature uses female imagery to depict Zion-Jerusalem-Israel (and other cities and nations) as blessed or condemned (Isa. 1:8; 37:22; 52:1-2; Mic. 4:8-13; Hos. 1-2). The prophet Amos blames wealthy people, both male and female, for oppressing the poor and making them suffer (2:6-7; 4:1-3).

The Religious Life of Women

Although the Old Testament more often focuses on the religious life of men, women were actively involved in religious expression. Hannah prayed (1 Sam. 1:9-13; 2:1-10, 18-20). Miriam led a spontaneous worship service of song and dance in praise of the Lord, who had brought them across the Red Sea (Exod. 15:20). Hagar and Samson's mother received messages from God's angels (Gen. 16; 21; Judg. 13).

Women were expected to remember the instructions God had given to Israel and follow them (Ezra 9:2-3). Leaders were concerned about Israelite men who married non-Israelite women (1 Kings 11; Ezra 10; Neh. 13). Thus the faithfulness of husbands and children was closely connected to the faithfulness of their wives and mothers, or even dependent on faith of the women (Neh. 13:23-27).

Jeremiah 44 indicates that some Israelite women exiled in Egypt were devoted to a female deity called "the queen of heaven." The queen of heaven was also worshiped by men, as 44:17 makes clear. These women thought the fall of Judah and the exile happened because they had stopped bringing offerings to the queen of heaven. To prevent further tragedy, they resumed the rituals in exile.

God and Gender

Gender in the Old Testament extends to questions about God. The Bible is clear that God is a sexless being. Yet because the Scriptures frequently use male imagery and metaphor for God, people came to think of God as being male. Female metaphors and imagery for God in the Bible are frequently overlooked (for example, Isa. 66:13). This happens out of ignorance or to reinforce masculine imagery.

Theologically significant statements on this issue appear in Exodus 3:14 and 20:3-5. In 3:14, God gives a self-identification. When Moses asks God how the Deity wants to be known, God answers not in a noun, proper or common, which required the choice of grammatical gender in the Hebrew language. Instead, God uses a genderless first-person common singular verb, "I am who I am," and "I am."

Exodus 20:4-5b prohibits the worship of gods other than God and prohibits the construction of images of God.

"You shall not make for yourself an image or a likeness of anything that is in the sky above, or on the earth below, or in the water that is under the earth. You shall not bow down to them, and you shall not serve them" (translation mine).

There is a danger in using solely male language, imagery, and metaphors because it can lead to a violation of this commandment. God is not to be imaged as a human male or female or as any other created being. God makes it clear that Yahweh (the Lord) is not limited to human reality, and this is reinforced throughout the Bible.

To summarize, females and males both share the divine image and are created fully equal. Moreover, the role of women in the Old Testament is more nuanced than one would expect from what most of us heard in the teaching and preaching of the church in times past. Women did occupy leadership positions, though to a lesser extent than men and perhaps to a greater extent than a quick perusal of the text might indicate.

From the stories we do have, we know that women played a crucial role at critical times in Israel. The religious life of women was vibrant, and they were expected to be familiar with God's teachings.

Finally, the clear prohibition against creating images of God that are cast in human form should lead us to rethink our language and visual images of God.

What Do You Think?

1. Have you ever thought about the role women play in Old Testament stories? Were you surprised by what you've read here?

2. How might stories of women be part of the study and worship life of the church? How has the omission of such stories been harmful to men and women?

3. Should the church develop language and images of God that are without gender, to conform to the prohibition against images and likenesses of God taken from the created world?

4. In the Old Testament time period, the Law assumed that women tell the truth about rape. When did this change? Why?

5. Is the religious life of women different from the religious life of men in the modern world? Do men and women understand and look for God in different ways?

If You Want to Read More

Bird, Phyllis. *Missing Persons and Mistaken Identities: Women and Gender in Ancient Israel.* Fortress, 1997.

Day, Peggy L. *Gender and Difference in Ancient Israel.* Fortress, 1989.

LaCocque, André. *The Feminine Unconventional.* Fortress, 1990.

Trible, Phyllis. *God and the Rhetoric of Sexuality.* Fortress, 1978.

_____. *Texts of Terror.* Fortress, 1984.

Weems, Renita. *Just a Sister Away.* LuraMedia, 1988.

2

Gender in the New Testament

Adelia Neufeld Wiens

Adelia Neufeld Wiens, Winnipeg, Manitoba, is a spouse, mother, freelance writer, and calligrapher. She has a master's degree in religion from the University of Manitoba, and has occasionally taught biblical studies courses at the University of Manitoba and Canadian Mennonite Bible College. Adelia is married to Werner Wiens, and they have two children, Caleb and Ellen.

TWENTY YEARS ago, when I was in grade eleven at a Christian high school, I volunteered along with several other male students to take a turn speaking at one of our daily chapels. Oddly enough, all the boys were scheduled to speak, but I was never given a date.

I didn't let this bother me much. The next year, when I became chair of the "Devotional Committee," I simply scheduled a date for myself. Soon a staff member quizzed me about what I would be speaking on and about "how well prepared"

I was. Only then did I realize that I had been intentionally missed the previous year because of my sex.

Many other girls and women around the world have experienced prejudice much more blatant than that. They have not been able to get around it as easily as I did.

There have always been women in history who have tried to minister alongside men in the church. In the last several decades, people have shown more openness to the equality of men and women. So the issue of women's role in the church has gathered great momentum. Many people have tried to address this delicate, difficult, painful, and sometimes threatening task.

In the next few pages, I will review some aspects of the New Testament that provide glimpses into understanding the issues and arguments surrounding the topic of gender.

Where do I, the author of this chapter, stand? I believe that God created men and women equally, in the divine image, and God expects for each of us to do the best that we are able. I believe Jesus called women and men to be his disciples and "feed his sheep." I believe the Holy Spirit works within us to create a nurturing, healing, and challenging community. My position is that of a Christian feminist firmly committed to the church.

The New Testament World

In New Testament times, there was a convergence of many cultural influences—Greek, Roman, Oriental, Jewish, and more. While Jesus and Paul were Jewish, the impact of Gentile culture left its mark on their society. Thus Jesus was not only a threat to the Jewish establishment, but also to the Roman political rulers. In addition, there are several tax-collector stories in the New Testament that give us a glimpse of the foreign powers that were to be obeyed. Further, Paul's letters are addressed to several different cultural groups, including Jews, Romans, and Greeks.

For the Greeks, women were given somewhat higher

respect than in some other societies. Plato vigorously affirmed the equality of the sexes. Aristotle, on the other hand, viewed women's nature as inferior. In everyday life, women lived in seclusion, for it was considered improper for men to take their wives out in public.

In Rome, women were treated with somewhat more openness. Legally, however, the woman was still regarded as a piece of property under the control of her husband. Among the Jews during the time of Jesus and Paul, women continued to be subject to patriarchal systems. They had the status of inferiors. The female child was less desirable than a male child. In the home, though, the woman's position was one of dignity.

In the area of religious obligations, women were not given much opportunity to participate as leaders. In public, rabbis were not allowed to greet or speak to women. At the synagogue, women were separated from men and not allowed to read aloud or to take part in any leading function.

The theology of Judaism, however, gave women a guaranteed standing before God as co-heirs of the covenant. They participated in all the religious festivals, attended religious gatherings, and shared in sacrificial meals. A woman could never serve as a priest, though. Her ritual uncleanness and her sexual nature made this taboo.

In all three cultures, Greek, Roman, and Jewish, it was assumed that the man was the head of the house, and that the woman owed the man obedience.

Jesus and Gender

Much is made of the fact that Jesus chose twelve males as his disciples. In the Catholic church, this fact is used to justify the argument that priesthood is only for males.

Nevertheless, Jesus was also surrounded by women who wanted to follow him. The Gospels have many stories about Jesus and his relationships with women. He visited Mary and Martha (Luke 10:38-42) and the Samaritan woman at the well

(John 4:7-29). He healed the woman with the issue of blood (Mark 5:25-34) and appeared to Mary Magdalene, who is the first to see the risen Lord (John 20:11-18).

Jesus did not reject women known to be sinners but enabled them to experience forgiveness (Luke 7:36-50). He accepted women who are foreigners (John 4:7-42). Jesus observed the plight of widows who didn't have male relatives or guardians (Mark 12:38-44; Luke 7:11-17; 18:2-5).

He had great regard for the actions of women. Jesus took seriously the ways in which Mary and Martha responded to him, admonishing Martha to leave aside her work and be with him (Luke 10:38-42). Jesus' teachings were often given in a context where both men and women were present. Women and men traveled with him as companions (Luke 8:1-3; Mark 15:40-41).

For both women and men, Jesus describes a new morality which turns the old law on its head. Thus Jesus defines adultery more broadly than the carefully constructed Jewish laws. He says, "Everyone who looks at a woman with lust has already committed adultery with her in his heart" (Matt. 5:28). Suddenly the man is held responsible not only for the actions of his body, but also for the thoughts of his mind. He may no longer indulge in fantasies that threaten the dignity of another woman.

Throughout his life Jesus challenged cultural stereotypes by modeling a way of being male in his society. He was a man who in public cared for women and outcasts. Jesus was interested in children. He rejected the seductive power of status; he modeled the value of being a servant rather than a master (Luke 22:25-27; John 13:14).

Paul and Gender

For many centuries, the apostle Paul has been used as the major justification for the subordination of women in the church. Paul has provided the most explicit statements regarding the role of women, but people explain his writings in various ways. Some take him as a male chauvinist, and others as a speaker for the liberation of women.

It is not helpful to pin either label on him—*chauvinist* or *feminist*. We need to recognize Paul as a complex person, a man of conflict, caught in the tension of patriarchal tradition on one hand, and the freedom brought by Christ on the other.

Let us look at some of the words that Paul wrote.

> I want you to understand that Christ is the head of every man, and the husband is the head of his wife, and God is the head of Christ. (1 Cor. 11:3)

While many readers react most strongly to the words, "the husband is the head of his wife," this passage is in fact not likely to provide ammunition for suppression of women. The word for *head* in Greek is *kephalē,* better translated as *source.* Perhaps this passage is then an early Christian treatment of Genesis 2, where Jesus is interposed as the agent of creation, and thus is the *source* of man (1 Cor. 11:3). Thus, the man's source is Christ. Since woman was made from the man's rib, it follows woman's source is man. No subordination of woman to man is intended; it is simply an expression of the order of creative events.

The larger context of this passage allows us to see that Paul understands the church as having the interdependence of the body, as described in 1 Corinthians 12. No part of the body is subordinate; each is essential to the whole. There is a mutual, reciprocal relationship between a man and a woman, which is wholly subordinated to God (11:11-12). Both women and men pray and prophesy in the gatherings (11:4-5).

> As in all the churches of the saints, women should be silent in the churches. For they are not permitted to speak, but should be subordinate, as the law also says. If there is anything they desire to know, let them ask their husbands at home. For it is shameful for a woman to speak in church. (1 Cor. 14:33b-35)

The major emphasis here is on noise control. The verses just prior to this text show that several are talking at once, making much noise but little meaning (1 Cor. 14:26-33). Paul asks that all speaking be interpreted in a meaningful way. If there is no one to make sense of the utterance, then the speaker is to remain silent (14:28). Catherine Clark Kroeger observes that Paul is writing to a Greco-Roman congregation. So the cultural and religious context of the Greco-Roman world becomes crucial:

> The religious practices of women in the ancient world were often indecent, indecorous and indiscreet. Men feared their rites, hated them, derided them, and repudiated them. What happened when pagan women were converted and incorporated into the worshiping body of Jesus Christ? (14; see list below)

Thus Paul may be responding to a cultural context where women, accustomed to noisy and abandoned worship, are now joining the church and behaving in a disorderly manner. In his strong words, Paul is calling for a corrective to their behavior.

Elsewhere, Paul's inclusivity is clear:

> There is no longer Jew or Greek, there is no longer slave or free, there is no longer male and female; for all of you are one in Christ Jesus. (Gal. 3:28)

The point of this passage is unity. This text is likely part of an early baptismal formula in the early church, and reflects its stance of equality. Paul knows there will continue to be distinctions among people, because people are different and have different gifts. Here, however, he destroys any value judgments made on the basis of such distinctions. This passage may justifiably be viewed as central to Paul's theology.

Women's Involvement in the Early Church

To the pious Jews of biblical times, it would have been scandalous to have women and men traveling and interacting together. As we saw above, however, women often traveled together in Jesus' entourage.

The documents of the early church reflect many places where women were present and actively participating. The churches of Paul accepted female as well as male leaders (Rom. 16:1, 3, 6-7, 12-13, 15). Paul writes of women who have "struggled beside me in the work of the gospel" (Phil. 4:2-3). Priscilla (Prisca) and Aquila are seen as equal partners in their ministry; in four out of six references, Priscilla is named first (Acts 18:2, 18, 26; 1 Cor. 16:19; Rom. 16:3; 2 Tim. 4:19).

Thus women were active and regarded highly in the early church. The Gospels, written late in the first century, often give significant standing to women usually seen as outcasts. Matthew, used as a teaching tool in the early church, gives a genealogy for Jesus. Though based on male descent, it includes names of four women besides Mary who were involved in some sexual irregularity: Rahab (a prostitute, Josh. 2:1), Tamar (had intercourse with her father-in-law, Gen. 38), Ruth (obtains her husband by using courtship customs acceptable at that time, Ruth 3:6-18), and Bathsheba (adulteress, 2 Sam. 11:2-5).

Further, Jesus was prepared to minister to outcast women and to welcome them into the kingdom of God. He said, "Truly, I tell you, the tax collectors and the prostitutes are going into the kingdom of God ahead of you [the chief priests and elders]" (Matt. 21:31).

Most interpreters doubt that this positive view of the role and nature of women is shared throughout the New Testament. The pastoral epistles, written around the end of the first century, have several sections where women are commanded to be submissive to their husbands (1 Tim. 2:11-12; Titus 2:5; compare Col. 3:18; Eph. 5:22; 1 Pet. 3:1-5).

There have been many attempts to provide helpful insights into these challenging texts (Schroeder, Schertz). But no matter how creative and compelling the interpretations are, it cannot be denied that women are presented as needing considerable guidance.

These are difficult passages for feminists to read. We may find a parallel in how hard it must have been for slaves to hear the words, "Slaves, accept the authority of your masters with all deference, not only those who are kind and gentle but also those who are harsh. For it is a credit to you if, being aware of God, you endure pain while suffering unjustly" (1 Pet. 2:18-19). These words may also be hurtful to those who have experienced family violence.

Eventually, the discussion on such texts comes down to the question, "How do we understand the authority of the Bible in our lives?" Many feminist biblical scholars have struggled over this.

Letty M. Russell, a pastor and biblical scholar, has grappled with this issue:

> The Bible has authority in my life because it makes sense of my experience and speaks to me about meaning and purpose of my humanity in Jesus Christ. In spite of its ancient and patriarchal worldviews, in spite of its inconsistencies and mixed messages, the story of God's love affair with the world leads me to a vision of New Creation that impels my life. . . . [The Bible's] authority in my life stems from its story of God's invitation to participation in the restoration of wholeness, peace, and justice in the world. (138)

First we can look at the larger message of the Bible—reconciliation with God, salvation, hope, the kingdom present, the saving work of Jesus. Then we are able to place some of the puzzling words about women's roles into their historical context and acknowledge that times have changed. Just as we no longer justify slavery, we can no longer justify the suppression of women's voices who are helping us along the path of Christian discipleship and obedience.

Conclusion

In Galatians 6:2, Paul admonishes the readers, "Bear one another's burdens, and in this way you will fulfill the law of Christ." The issue of gender in the New Testament is a burden for many people within our churches. It will not do the kingdom of God any good if we ignore the challenges being presented to us by people who want to walk with us along the journey of faith. Let us continue to grapple with the questions, and ease the load for each other through encouragement, kindness, and gentleness.

What do you think?

1. Based on the Gospel accounts, how do you think Jesus would perceive gender issues today?

2. What is the most troublesome passage about gender issues in the New Testament for you? Why?

3. What is the most helpful passage about gender issues in the New Testament for you? Why?

4. How is the Bible authoritative in your life?

5. Read the story of Jesus and the Samaritan woman (John 4:5-29, 39-42). What does this account teach us about conversion and discipleship?

If You Want to Read More

Bushnell, Katherine C. *God's Word to Women*. 1923.
Repr., God's Word to Women Publishers.

Clark, Elizabeth A. *Women in the Early Church*. Michael Glazier, 1983.

Fraser, Elouise Renich, and Louis A. Kilgore. *Making Friends with the Bible*. Herald Press, 1995.

Keyes, Mardi. *Feminism and the Bible*. InterVarsity, 1995.

Kroeger, Catharine Clark. "A Classicist Looks at the Difficult Passages." In *Perspectives on Feminist Hermeneutics.* Occasional Papers, no. 10. Elkhart, Ind.: Inst. of Mennonite Studies, 1987.

Russell, Letty, ed. *Feminist Interpretation of the Bible.* Westminster, 1985.

Scanzoni, Letha Dawson, and Nancy Hardesty. *All We're Meant to Be: Biblical Feminism for Today.* Eerdmans, 1992.

Schertz, Mary. " 'Likewise You Wives . . .': Another Look at 1 Peter 2:11—5:11." *In Perspectives* (see above).

Schroeder, David. "The New Testament Haustafel: Egalitarian or Status Quo?" In *Perspectives* (see above).

Swidler, Leonard. *Biblical Affirmations of Women.* Westminster, 1979.

3

Gender and Sex Differences: Real or Imagined?

Ken and Irma Fast-Dueck

Irma and Ken Fast-Dueck live in Winnipeg, where they attend Bethel Mennonite Church. Irma has worked in pastoral ministry and is currently teaching practical theology at Canadian Mennonite Bible College. Ken teaches physical education at an elementary school. They are the parents of a son named Zachary.

ARE WOMEN and men different in more ways than their physical bodies? We have alternatively celebrated and struggled with gender differences. Ken is good at math and science. He's good at problem solving. When the vacuum cleaner doesn't work, he takes it apart systematically and figures out what is wrong. Irma becomes frustrated when she takes things apart and puts them back together. She loves literature and enjoys reading, quilting, and expressing herself in many other creative ways.

Ken likes to focus on details; Irma prefers to look at the bigger picture. Irma defines herself first through her relationships: wife, friend, teacher, daughter, sister. Ken defines himself first through his gifts and accomplishments: university degrees, work experience, musical ability, athletic prowess.

Irma is verbal. She likes to talk, and when there is a conflict, she wants to talk it out immediately. She knows what she's feeling and can express her feelings easily. She quickly gets frustrated when Ken needs time to think before working out a conflict. He needs time to reflect on his feelings.

Ken views sexual intimacy as a way of "connecting" with Irma and a good way to relieve stress and tension. When Irma feels "disconnected" from Ken, she needs to feel connected with him first through conversation and time together, before enjoying sexually intimate acts. When she is under stress, the last thing she wants is sexual intimacy!

The questions surrounding gender and sex differences are difficult to explore. These questions often lead to even more questions, many of which do not have answers. In many ways, how we look at such a topic is as important as the topic itself.

While we are not experts in this field, we have a keen interest in trying to understand who we are as male and female, individually and together. We will explore this topic from at least two perspectives: a social-psychological perspective, and a biblical-theological perspective.

Are There Real Differences (Other Than Biological Ones)?
Do the differences between us arise out of our separate genders, or are they merely personality differences? And if these differences are indeed gender differences, where do they come from? Are men and women socialized to think and act differently, or do those differences grow out of our particular physiology, innate from our creation?

It is helpful to think of male-female differences in two

ways: as gender differences, and as sex differences. Some researchers (psychologists, scientists, theologians) have found it helpful to distinguish between these. Sex refers to our genetic predispositions; gender identifies how socialization shapes who we are (Ashbrook, 174; see list below).

Many researchers concentrate on finding real differences. Do men and women differ in ways beyond gender (socialized) differences, or beyond obvious biological differences? For many years people have assumed that there are significant differences between women and men.

Theologians, scientists, psychologists, sociologists, and anthropologists claimed to find differences (beyond biological ones) and prove them through their respective disciplines. However, there is little agreement on why women and men are different. Are these characteristics gender differences or sex differences?

A scientific approach tends to separate the body from the mind. Such a separation of body and mind allows one to ask whether we are more than biologically different, and we must be careful of the assumptions behind such a question.

We believe that body and mind do not function independently of one another but rather as a seamless unity. We have totally different experiences of coming to maturity in a male or in a female body. This certainly affects our thinking and behaving, and we cannot even imagine otherwise. Thus, we support the idea that there are sex differences as well as gender differences.

We have tried to be more critical of certain gender differences which have been imposed upon us through socialization. Yet we often find it difficult to distinguish them from more genuine sex differences. In her book *In a Different Voice*, Carol Gilligan suggests that we develop "different voices" as women and men, because we inherit different genes and are shaped by different gender patterns. Both socialization and genetics need to be considered in reflecting on the differences between women and men.

So what have the scientists found to be male and female characteristics? If Ken were considered the typical male, the studies say he would have the following profile: Physically he would be taller than Irma (true), heavier than Irma (no comment), and more muscular (uncertain).

There would be no significant difference in general intelligence. Ken would do well on tests of mathematical reasoning and in spatial-visual tasks (requiring one to visualize objects in space).

In our personalities, there would be no significant differences in how sociable, empathic, and dependent we would be. In the area of confidence, Ken would more likely take credit for success or blame himself for failure. He would also be more aggressive in public and physically aggressive even when he wasn't angry. In values and moral judgments, he might emphasize justice, fairness, and individual rights.

On the other hand, Irma would get sick less often and live longer than Ken. In terms of manual dexterity, she would be faster. She would acquire language sooner and excel in verbal creativity tests. She would be no more nurturing and susceptible to influence than Ken would be. She might be more likely to emphasize care, human attachments, and a balance conflicting responsibilities in her value or moral framework.

When we look at the differences, the number of substantial traits is rather limited, yet they do exist, on average. However, some researchers argue that the differences noted above are influenced by biases in testing and procedures. Even scientists are affected by stereotypes.

People develop stereotypes to predict the behavior of others. In some instances, this can be a positive thing. But when placed in the context of male-female traits, this has traditionally caused a significant imbalance in terms of career choices, family responsibilities, and how males and females relate to each other.

We have just experienced the joy of having our first

child, and it has been interesting, noting how at an early age, gender is a significant issue. Of the initial phone calls we made, the first question asked was whether it was a boy or a girl, even before questions of appearance, weight, or health.

At birth, scientists have tried to note any sex differences. In their quest, some researchers have come to the conclusion that it is impossible to guess the sex of a newborn baby simply from watching how it behaves. Sex differences clearly emerge somewhat later in life. If our son were wearing pink, researchers report that he would be held more often than if he were wearing boy colors. Adults sex stereotype children at an early age. If such stereotypes are experienced by children this early and this subtly, is it any doubt that gender differences show up?

The question of nature or nurture will not be easily resolved. Virtually every study done on sex and gender differences returns to this debate. Since we recognize researcher bias (conscious or subconscious), it is quite difficult for us to distinguish sex and gender differences. Perhaps the question is not so much why there are differences, but how we respond to differences. We each must deal with the "baggage" we have been given, whether it is biological or socialized.

Biblical-Theological Perspectives

What does the Bible say about sex and gender differences? We may be disappointed to find that the Scriptures do not offer direct answers to our questions about sex differences. The scientific nature-versus-nurture debate is not argued on the pages of our biblical text. However, the Bible does help us to reflect more theologically on ourselves as female and male.

First, while the Bible helps us understand our identities as women and men, this is done in the context of a larger community identity. In other words, in the biblical story (especially in the Old Testament), questions of individual identity are less important than one's identity within a particular community.

Rather than asking one identity question, "Who am I as a male or female?" the Bible asks other questions: "Who am I as a male or female in the context of this community?" Or even more typical, "Who are we in the context of this community?" The question of sex differentiation is a contemporary question influenced by our more individualistic society, and it is difficult to ask the question in a biblical context. The Bible challenges us to know ourselves more fully in relationship with others.

Second, understanding that God is neither male nor female helps us in understanding ourselves as male and female. For the Israelites of the Old Testament, it was significant that sexuality was not associated with the divine. The Canaanite Baal cults surrounding the Israelites were fertility religions which celebrated creation as the result of the union of male and female deities.

For the Israelites, the radical exclusion of sexuality from divinity placed sexuality into the human realm where humanity could have control of it. We are not helpless victims of fertility gods whom we must appease. Instead, we have the power to choose how we will live together. Even though sexuality was separate from the Creator, it was considered a gift of Creation and essentially good. It is sad and perverse that for centuries the church has seen sexuality as less than good.

Finally, our Bible reminds us that we are first and primarily human, and in the second place, we are female and male. There is more holding us together as male and female in our common humanity than there is separating us. The Creation accounts of Genesis 1–3 are the most obvious resource to help us reflect on the meaning of being male and female. In both accounts of the creation of male and female (1:26-27; 2:7-25), male and female are clearly one—and two.

In the first account, male and female are created at the same time. "So God created humankind in his image, in the image of God he created them; male and female he created them" (Gen. 1:27). The Hebrew word for *humankind* is *adam,* used in both Creation accounts; it is neither the proper name *Adam* nor a collective emphasizing men as a group. Instead, *adam* is a generic term meaning human being, humankind, humanity. When humankind is divided into male and female, a different Hebrew term is used: *ish* (male) and *ishshah* (female). The woman is *adam* just as the man is *adam.*

Thus the *image of God* refers neither to the man alone nor the woman alone; it is shared by both together. The image of God is found in their common humanity.

The same holds true with the word *adam* in the second account of the creation of male and female, in Genesis 2:7-25. In this text God forms *adam* from the dust of the ground. Here there is a little play on the words: the word for ground or earth is *adamah.* So God creates *adam* from the *adamah,* which literally translates as the *earthling* from the *earth* (2:7). Again, women and men share a common humanity in the creation of *adam.* Only later (2:23) do they become male and female (*ish* and *ishshah*; for in-depth discussion, see Trible, listed below).

Our Bible reminds us of the common humanity which we share as women and men. It also reminds us that our maleness and femaleness are integral to understanding what it is to be human. We are two and yet one. Celia Allison Hahn calls this tension a *sexual paradox.* We need to find a balance between the fact that we are created "male and female" and that we are also "all one." Hahn uses the word paradox to point to that which cannot be explained logically but which moves us into the mystery of the divine and of Creation (11).

Closing Reflections: Does it Matter?

We believe that gender does matter. We recognize that we share much as women and men. Yet if we deny our differences, we reduce the richness of our life together. We have appreciated the feminist movement in its stress on differing experiences of women and men. This awareness has helped to bring greater equality and understanding between the sexes.

Sadly, equality has often been equated with sameness. With this has come the tendency to downplay our differences, as if any admission of sex difference is evidence of inferiority, or may be taken that way. (Society rarely attributes inferiority to men, even though women usually outlive them!) Sexual differentiation is therefore seen as a threat to equality.

We believe we can be equal *and* different. This is not to suggest that women and men should be limited in the roles in which they function. Instead, we need to recognize that even within those roles, we will function in different ways by virtue of our sex. Acknowledging our differences allows us to experience the rich contributions of women and men.

The challenge of gender relations is one of the most urgent issues of our time. We hope that as believers we learn to live uniquely and compassionately in our oneness.

What Do You Think?

1. Do you think women and men are different in ways other than what is determined by their physical bodies?

2. How have stereotypes about gender affected you and your choices in life?

3. Men and women are both created in God's image. Is this the perspective with which you were raised?

4. How can the church affirm our gender differences without restricting roles for men and women?

If You Want to Read More

Ashbrook, James B. "Different Voices, Different Genes: 'Male and Female Created God Them.'" *Journal of Pastoral Care* 46/2 (summer 1992).

Gilligan, Carol. *In a Different Voice: Psychological Theory and Women's Development.* Harvard University Press, 1982.

Hahn, Celia. *Sexual Paradox: Creative Tensions in Our Lives and in Our Congregations.* Pilgrim Press, 1991.

Tannen, Deborah. *Talking from 9 to 5.* Morrow, 1994.

_____. *You Just Don't Understand: Women and Men in Conversation.* Ballantine Books, 1990.

Trible, Phyllis. *God and the Rhetoric of Sexuality.* Fortress, 1978.

4

Homemaking and Careers: Cooking the Ordinary Soup of Our Everyday Lives

Eileen Klassen Hamm with Les Klassen Hamm

Eileen and Les Klassen Hamm live in Saskatoon, Saskatchewan. Part of the week, Eileen works as coordinator of the Women's Concerns Program for MCC Saskatchewan. Other days she spends most of her time caring for her children, Simon and Emily. Les is pastor at Wildwood Mennonite Church. Each received a master of divinity degree from Associated Mennonite Biblical Seminary.

I, EILEEN, enjoy making soups. In fact, I even delight in it. There's something quite amazing about how a simmering soup pot embraces our home with its aroma, enticing friends and family into the kitchen. Soup is nourishing and comforting, and it's loved by young and old. Also, soup is flexible; soup recipes are incredibly tolerant and will indulge the most creative and even experimental cooks.

In a pinch, soup can be used as a metaphor for how we mix together the various fragments of our lives. This chapter is intended to help us discuss how we balance the various tasks of homemaking and careers. We will explore these tasks through a description of cooking a well-made soup that becomes a sturdy and heartwarming meal, making good use of resources.

As we reflect on many aspects of homemaking and careers, I invite you to throw gender issues into the cooking process. What are our expectations of the women in our lives? What are our expectations of the men in our lives? Discussions of gender roles and relationships become poignant when they touch the very heart of who we are. The tasks of making homes and developing careers are central to our understandings of who we are and what we seek in life. What are we, as women and men, seeking through our careers and our homemaking?

Let's look carefully at the basic ingredients of homemaking and careers. What exactly are we talking about? In our family, homemaking includes caring about relationships: practicing hospitality with family and friends, making time for good conversations, developing strong bonds with spouse and children, giving gifts, writing letters. Homemaking also includes maintaining our house, yard, and garden: washing dishes, doing laundry, cleaning the house, mowing grass, transplanting tomatoes, buying groceries, paying bills, weeding.

Perhaps the most exhausting and rewarding task of homemaking for us at present is caring for two small children. Some families care for older children, elderly relatives, or persons with disabilities. Caregiving includes many small and immediate tasks, often performed many times each day or week.

Careers will include some similar kinds of activities. For instance, many kinds of work involve repeating tasks several or many times: accountants prepare numerous tax forms, carpenters build similar houses, teachers guide many students through the same learning process, doctors look in many children's ears for infections. Most careers also include a relational component and require us to develop relational skills to be used with colleagues or customers.

I see two significant differences between careers and homemaking. (1) Careers are most often lived out in public, while many tasks of homemaking occur in a more private sphere. (2) Homemaking is not rewarded with societal prestige or a wage (unless you are working in another person's home). These dynamics play a part in how women and men experience careers and homemaking, and how women and men relate to each other as we carry out our many tasks.

Given these ingredients, how will we cook this life soup?

The Recipe: Seeking Shalom

Most of us who cook soup will read a recipe or several recipes before we begin to throw things into the soup pot. The recipes serve as a guide, the passing on of experience, a wise reminder, an image of the end product.

As we gather up the fragments of our everyday lives and try to cook up a balanced lifestyle amid developing careers and making homes, we benefit from wise reminders of what we are seeking. The theme of shalom resonates throughout the Bible, reflecting God's hope and promise for people.

In my seminary studies, the Hebrew textbook translated *shalom* as "peace, welfare, wholeness." This seems to be a fairly solid and encompassing base from which to examine our ordinary lives. God's invitation to shalom challenges us to peace in our many relationships—with family, self, community, earth. God's invitation to shalom challenges us to wholeness—emotional, spiritual, social, physical, and mental. God's invitation to shalom challenges us to seek the welfare of the community.

Are the recipes we are following in our lives creating shalom? In our balancing of homemaking and careers, are we reflecting shalom between women and men? Many if not all of us have been influenced by unhealthy recipes. These recipes suggest that men will receive satisfaction from providing financially for their family, even if they hate their job, and women will receive satisfaction from taking care of everyone, even if they also spend a large portion of time doing work for pay.

However, if men don't learn to know their children, and women can't explore their potential, where is shalom? It is sometimes agonizingly difficult to find shalom. Cultural stereotypes and subtle social and family pressures sometimes compromise our ability to make wise choices. Can we free our imaginations to create new recipes that will bring health for each of us and all of us together?

The Cooks: Mutuality and Collaboration

There is this old adage that says, "Too many cooks spoil the broth." I would like to refute this maxim or at least qualify it. Many cooks only spoil things if they are not communicating and working together. We—women and men, young and old—are in this life together, and we have much to offer each other. How will we produce an abundant and wholesome soup for all? Through mutuality and collaboration.

Through mutual love, care, and trust, we can sustain healthy relationships and provide healthy contexts into which we invite others. Mutuality urges women and men toward growing interdependence and partnership. God provides a model by freely becoming a partner with people. Jesus, too, calls us into a relationship of trust and participation, by reaching out to restore shalom for individuals and communities. Mutuality has consequences for women and men learning to cook together. We certainly do not all have to cook the same way, or even cook the same things, but we all need to have access to the "kitchen" and receive authentic respect for our contributions.

One of the ways we can demonstrate relationships of mutuality is through collaboration. In the writing of this chapter, I looked to my partner, Les, for collaboration. As we brainstormed ideas and discussed our goals and struggles around homemaking and careers, we shaped the framework for this chapter. It is a broader discussion than I would have created on my own. We, women and men, need to recognize each others' life-giving activities, and struggle together for shalom, for wholeness. So we will collaborate. Like good cooks, we recognize the rightness and the energy within each others' abilities when we sample the unique and tantalizing flavors we can create together.

Balancing Ingredients: Homes, Work, Relationships, Spirituality

Now, how shall we mutually and collaboratively work at balancing careers and homemaking such that we bring shalom to our lives and other lives that touch ours? Is such a thing possible?

There is no one right way to make a pot of soup. Some of us use cups and spoons to measure, some use hands and pinches. Some of us need a lot of time to make soup, because we have helpers with little hands. Some of us barely have time to pour boiling water over instant noodles.

I will not suggest an answer to the work of balancing the tasks of homemaking and careers. Many factors affect these tasks: family needs, geography, family structure, job markets, age, community support, education, poverty, or wealth. The balancing act is ultimately dynamic. Yet amid the complex ingredients of our lives, I believe we need to seek the broader perspective of shalom—of peace, welfare, and wholeness.

In my view, the following ingredients are significant aspects of a healthy, wholesome life: homes, work, relationships, and spirituality.

Our *homes* are the context within which the rest of our life's ingredients come together. Homes have the potential to be healthy contexts for us. Homes can surround us and provide us with stability. They send us off and welcome us back again. Homes can provide safety and security for us and our families. They may provide a space for some of our closest relationships. I trust that we can be our most authentic selves in our homes.

Healthy homes have the ability to comfort and to challenge us, from infancy into adolescence, from young adulthood into elderhood. Our homes can be places to learn and to practice good stewardship of the earth's resources. Homes provide a space from which to offer hospitality, and to reach out into our wider communities.

Not all of our homes are healthy and safe spaces. The tasks of making good and supportive homes are many and time-consuming, especially if our homes include small children, elderly people, or persons with disabilities. The tasks of making healthy homes are, however, extremely rewarding and life-giving when they are based on relationships of mutuality. How can we better collaborate on the responsibilities of homemaking so that we can maintain high standards of personal and familial well-being?

Our *work* is also important in developing our identities; it can give meaning to our lives. Some of the work we do is for wages, some not for wages. Some of our work has a clear job description; other work is more difficult to define. But whether we are spending time teaching, cooking, running a business, nursing, helping an elder parent with household tasks, volunteering in the church and/or community, studying, farming, cleaning up after small children, or doing whatever—we have the potential to work toward wholeness for ourselves and others.

The work we do provides us with diverse experiences and connections. I'm assuming that we all do more than one kind of work. The diversity of our work provides us with a livelihood (hopefully!) and larger circles of communities with which to relate. The diversity also enriches our life soup.

I realize here that I have made the line between home-making and careers rather fluid (as soups generally are!). I believe that for some people, homemaking is a career. It is a career they have chosen and at which they are highly skilled. However, I also believe that in relationships of mutuality, we do not take anyone's work for granted, whether it is for a pay-check or not. We will be open to adjusting work choices as our individual needs change.

Think about your work. Do you have too much paying work and not enough volunteer work? Do you have too much volunteer work? Do you have too much boring work and not enough meaningful work? Do you have so much meaningful work that you can't swallow it all? What identity are you cook-ing up for yourself?

God created us to live in mutuality with each other, and I will suggest that our *relationships* with people are the seasonings in our soup. Our relationships provide diverse flavors and aro-mas in our lives, and they add spice to our characters. How do our relationships provide for people's welfare or well-being? By loving each other, we pronounce each other's worth. We treat our relationships with care because we recognize the fragility of the human spirit along with the strength of human love.

Around homemaking and careers, we make many choices: Who goes out to work? Who works from home? How much income do we need? Our view of our relationships should influence these choices. What do we want for our children, ourselves, our parents, our community?

Seasonings take time to flavor our soups. It also takes time to live with people, learn to know them, and let them know us. Is there time in our lives for relationships—easy relationships, difficult relationships, long-term relationships? Are we willing to taste new flavors? Cilantro? What's that?

The final ingredient in our hearty life soup is spirituali-ty. I will liken our spirituality to the time it takes to make good soup. A mystique surrounds good cooking. That's why you find instructions like this: "Simmer till done."

God brings connections of meaning between the ingredients in our lives, even when those ingredients resist linking. God provides us a spiritual energy to help integrate our homes, our work, and our relationships. Faith journeys take time to unfold. God is with us through the making of our lives.

The Taste Test: Who Is Being Served?

In our life right now, our soup includes a full-time paying job for Les, a part-time voluntary service job for me, a four-year-old son and a one-year-old daughter, and significant friendships. We have chosen to keep our living expenses below one full-time salary, to remain flexible with childcare as well as jobs.

This combination of activities and relationships has served us fairly well. However, Les would still like a little more time for living and playing with our children, and I would like some more responsibilities away from home. At the same time, we recognize the privileges we do have: a salary in a difficult economy, reasonably low living expenses, flexible work schedules, and an excellent support community.

The potential for healthy and wholesome soup is here. Homes can be places of safety that provide us with stability. Work can bring meaning and strong identity to our lives. Relationships can reflect our worth back to us. And spirituality can help us to integrate our experiences.

Nevertheless, cooking up good and wholesome soup is not simple. Various pressures combine to challenge the most adept soup makers: increasing work hours and expectations, diminishing job markets, domestic violence, dwindling government social programs, and gender discrimination. Do we have the courage and creativity to invite change, to adjust the recipes?

The government agency Statistics Canada reports that when government social programs are cut back, women are the ones who most often take on the responsibility for the additional nonpaid work, such as childcare or eldercare. What is our response? Many women continue to earn less than men for comparable work. Who is being served?

Many men struggle with job expectations coupled with greater desires to be more actively involved in homemaking and parenting. What can change? Work is required to bring justice and shalom to our lives, at home and in public.

I have asked many more questions than I have answered. This is partly because I have many questions in the midst of homemaking and career choices. It is also partly because I believe our discussions with each other around these questions will be much more helpful than any formula could ever be.

Striving toward good and healthy lifestyles for our communities and families is an ongoing process. I hope we all use our courage and creativity to adjust the recipes in our seeking after shalom.

What Do You Think?

1. What models for balancing homemaking and careers do you see among women and men in your church community? How are women and men being served by these models?

2. Compared to your home of origin, how is your balancing of homemaking and careers similar and different?

3. What stresses are you feeling right now in relation to career choices, homemaking, and caregiving? What choices do you have for changes? Who could help you identify choices or responses?

4. In your life soup, do you have time to savor relationships? Is there time for spirituality, to seek the meaning behind your experiences?

5. What do you like about your life soup? What would you like to change?

If You Want to Read More

Miller-McLemore, Bonnie J. *Also a Mother: Work and Family as Theological Dilemma.* Abingdon, 1994.

Mintz, Steven, and Susan Kellogg. *Domestic Revolutions: A Social History of American Family Life.* Free Press, 1988.

Okin, Susan Moller. *Justice, Gender and the Family.* Basic Books, 1989.

Patton, John, and Brian H. Childs. *Christian Marriage and Family: Caring for Our Generations.* Abingdon, 1988.

Van Leeuwen, Mary Stewart. *Gender and Grace: Love, Work and Parenting in a Changing World.* InterVarsity, 1990.

5

Living in Our Created Bodies

Karen Schlichting and Aiden Schlichting Enns

Karen Schlichting works at Project Peacemakers, an ecumenical action group in Winnipeg, Manitoba. Aiden Schlichting Enns works as conference editor for the Canadian Mennonite *periodical, and as a freelance writer and photographer. They have no children, but most of their siblings have more than one child, bringing the current total of nephews and nieces to sixteen. They are part of a household of four adults living as an intentional community, with a sophisticated cat named Edgar.*

IN WRITING about our bodies, we both decided to lower our guard and become as vulnerable as possible. As a result, some of what we say may shock and even offend some readers. Our intention is not to offend anyone. Rather, in talking openly about our stories, we hope others may be spared some of the painful secrecy, gnawing self-doubt, and feelings of uncleanness we experienced. We wish to celebrate the bodies our

Creator has given us, not simply to tolerate or ignore them.

Some may say the church is not a place to talk about bodily functions and experiences. But that silence (or taboo) can quickly lead to confusion and identity crises, especially among younger people. By avoiding the issue, we tend to bottle up feelings and urges until they come out in inappropriate or self-destructive ways. We hope that as we begin to talk openly with each other and in our church communities, we will have a greater appreciation for the goodness in each of us—not just goodness in our minds or spirits, but goodness in our bodies as well.

Her Thoughts

Over my thirty-one years of living, I have thought about my body numerous times and in a number of ways. I have, over the years, both liked and disliked the shape of my body. I've experienced a lot of physical pain with this body. I've wondered about my sex drive and what pleases me. I've also tried "body beautification" at various times.

My earliest recollection of bodily dissatisfaction was probably in grade five. I began to realize that my pants did not fit properly. I didn't fill them out in the right places (or in any places, for that matter). My legs hung like hockey sticks in my new Wrangler wide-leg jeans. My body was not like the ones in the Sears catalog.

As I grew older, the problem became worse. I remember being excited to find a section on dieting in one of my mother's *Good Housekeeping* cookbooks. It talked not about how to lose weight but how to *gain* weight. For the first time, I read something that validated my own experience. I realized I was not alone with my perceived problem. I discovered that the problem of having a body of incorrect thickness was common, and perhaps even an international issue. Yet I continued to think of myself in the same way.

Not only were my legs *the problem* and the *Good*

Housekeeping weight-gain diet *the solution*, but my hair was too straight and too dark, my face too blemished and pale, my teeth too far apart, and my body too hairy. Happily, there were solutions to all of these problems: I would simply have to perm, pluck, scour, roast, and shave my body, and all would be fine. I too could look like the young women in the Sears catalog. In those years, my body was the enemy. I wanted so badly for it to be different.

Not only were the external parts of my body the enemy; at age thirteen, the internal workings of my body gave me further disappointment. When I began menstruating, I realized I was doomed to be a woman. I remember hating being referred to as "a young woman." Those words evoked a quick and bitter response in me. I felt I had just been called a bad name. For several years, I kept my menstruation a secret. I wanted no one to know about this terrible, bloody, and painful thing happening to me, except for my mother (whom I told only for practical purposes).

My body had betrayed me. Every month it reminded me that I was now apart from my dad and my brother. Sadly, I perceived this separation as a negative thing. I moved from being like others—and worth the same as others—to being damaged, dirty, and stuck with carrying a big secret.

Religion and Culture

The Mennonite environment and culture of my youth was not much different from the culture and values portrayed in *Good Housekeeping* magazine. The facts were clear: I was not perfect; Barbie was perfect. As companions for the rest of my life, I would have to embrace "beauty products" made by Clairol, Neat, and Avon.

Yet my religious upbringing did manage to root in the back of my mind a thought that contradicted this dependence on beauty products. I believed God didn't really care about my imperfections. I felt that my disappointment and anger toward my body was even slapping God, my Creator, in the face. So as I gazed in the mirror with growing dissatisfaction, my guilt also increased.

How could I be so ungrateful for what God had given me? I was, after all, created in the image of God. So I valued these religious notions of self-acceptance and divine beauty. But they were outweighed by the realities of going to school and wanting to be accepted by my peers, and perhaps even catching the eye of a young man.

As I look at the Bible with my body in mind, I begin to ask questions. On one hand, the body is called the temple of God, and is meant to be kept clean and pure. But on the other hand, the female body is often equated with temptation, the whore, and the adulteress. I wonder where that comes from? I think it has to do with the fact that throughout the ages, women have been linked to things physical more than men.

Women have cycles of menstruation, and they have the capacity to carry, birth, and nurse children. Therefore, people have understood women to be closer to nature than men are. In patriarchal cultures, this close connection of (lowly) women to nature led to the glorification of the mind and intellect (supposedly the "masculine"). Mind was supposed to control and dominate the physical (the natural, wild, and "feminine").

On the positive side, God did create our bodies good. For example, God's incarnation as Jesus Christ unifies the split between body and spirit. The spirit and the body were fully realized in the Christ, and it was good.

Nevertheless, our religious teachings have tended to create a false separation between the mind or spirit and the body. The spirit is elevated and the body devalued. As this separation works its way into our thinking and being, we feel uncomfortable with our sexuality. We begin to suppress our sexual desires or sensations because we think they are dirty and bad, and defile our bodies, which are to be kept "pure" as God's holy temples.

Bodily Ignorance

As women, many of us have adopted feelings of disdain for the physical or we've avoided the physical altogether. I heard of a young Mennonite woman in southern Manitoba who was having awful stomach cramps. The family took her to the hospital and learned she was about to have a child. She was not even aware that she had conceived and had been carrying a child for the previous nine months. She obviously was not educated about the functions of her own body, and she lacked even the most basic instruction about sexual activity.

This young unmarried woman suffered the consequences of being part of a community in which the body was not even to be talked about. A shroud of secrecy covers our discussion about the body and sexuality. Thus I can easily imagine other situations among Mennonites where women are victims of abuse or incest. Because of religious taboos, women too often carry deep pain bottled up inside throughout life.

This example of sexual ignorance is an extreme form of what many of us experience in more subtle ways every day. Our church community encourages women to be silent about our bodies, and to ignore what our bodies are telling us. In the name of humility, women historically were encouraged to give up fancy dress and to pay little attention to how our bodies looked. It was also considered a virtue to ignore our own physical needs, whether that be for food or rest, and to tend to the physical needs of others.

This mentality is rarely explicitly spelled out, yet it is a powerful message. A woman is quietly praised if she works endlessly (as in Prov. 31), and is held suspect (or even despised) if she pauses to put her feet up, take a long bath, go for a walk, or work out in the gym. Often no one has to tell her that resting is wrong; her own conscience, conditioned by the community, tells her.

As people of God, we have a long way to go before we will without guilt be able to embrace our bodies—their shape, color, and sexuality. I think the spirit of God has much to give us in this regard. We do not want to exploit and feel guilty about our physical and sexual selves. Instead, we want to live more fully as God's creatures. So we need to reeducate ourselves and reread the Scriptures, paying more attention to women's experience and to gender issues.

I am happy to report that I no longer hate my body— thanks to the wisdom that comes with age, a good community, and supportive relationships. I have learned to listen to that small voice inside that tells me I'm okay, and my body is not my enemy. I've been able to accept menstruation as normal and healthy, and a positive expression of being woman. I can feel feminine and sexual without the help of Gillette shaving cream or Max Factor eyelash enhancers.

I'm trying to celebrate my natural shape and block out voices that tell me I'm not good enough as I am. Yet for women, those voices have a long history; they are on every street corner and fill the flyers that enter our homes day by day. We have difficult, ongoing work to connect with our bodies again, or maintain a connection, but it is well worth the effort.

His Thoughts

Looking back at how I have lived inside my body, I wonder why I went through a tight-pants phase. I recall washing and drying my jeans before going roller-skating with the church youth group. Once I had to lie on the ground to get my pants on. I couldn't get the zipper up unless I squirmed on the floor and sucked in my gut. That was about age 16. Now I'm 35, have been married for 9 years, have gained 30 pounds, and usually need a belt to keep my pants up.

In high school I felt uncomfortably secure with my body. My level of security seemed to be directly proportional to the size and strength of my muscles. In the weight room, I could bench press "the stack," and I would climb ropes or do multiple chin-ups to show others how strong I was. Maybe I wore tight clothes at this age to prove to myself and others that I had become a "man."

I remember using the terms *fem, fag, wimp* and *sissy,* to describe other boys who did not appear to be strong. As a young man, I gained my masculine identity according to how macho I could appear. For example, in grade nine I played rugby. That was cool because it was a quite physical game. We didn't have to wear any pads except a cup and a mouth guard. So we had to be tough to play, and I wanted to be tough. But I quit after only one year of playing. Why? Because I was afraid of the other boys hitting me. I played tennis instead.

After high school, I gradually became more comfortable with my body, although I still agonized over what jeans to buy. I wanted to look casual and yet cool. One time I tried on a purple, zebra-striped shirt and thought it was too small, but the young female clerk said, "Hey, if you've got it, flaunt it!" I didn't buy it—too shy. As I look back at that incident, the clerk's statement says something about our popular notion of bodies: Some people have it (beauty or good looks) and should show it off. Other people don't and therefore should hide their bodies.

Now I have come to realize that our world is a diverse place, with different kinds of bodies. Each of them worth the same. I have come to understand God as being reflected in this diversity.

Thorn in My Flesh

Living in my created body has at times caused me much grief. Like Paul in the Bible, I had "a thorn in my flesh." In my church youth group, I learned it was bad to masturbate. The leaders said or implied that God didn't like it. When I heard it was wrong, I was curious and wanted to try it. Nothing happened. It felt dumb, a little humiliating. I guess I was one of the minority of males (1 percent?) that didn't do it. A few years later, however, I discovered it was pleasing.

My confidence as a nice Christian young man was shaken by my uncontrollable urge to stimulate myself. It took several years to deal with the guilt, feelings of failure, and inadequacy that accompanied this behavior. As I look back at this period, which lasted into the early years of my marriage with Karen, I can see how much harm that understanding did to myself and to my partner.

I read some Christian literature on the topic of sexuality and shared my struggles with other men in a small group. From that, I came to a new understanding. I saw my desires as normal. I realized that I did not engage in unhealthy fantasizing nor exhibit obsessive behavior. I also learned the appropriate place for "self-care"—which sometimes is reading a book, buying a coffee, or engaging in "self-pleasuring."

My experience with my body is probably not average. Some men will not even understand the question, "How do you as a man experience your body?" Others have exercised more, gone on diets more, been more sexually active, or have wrestled more with sexual identity questions.

Indirect Lessons at Church

We have much in common as Mennonites—the influence of the church and the Bible on our lives. Except for a few lectures on sex and dating in our youth group, I heard little talk about body issues. Indirectly, however, the church taught me volumes.

In some ways, the church sent me messages similar to the predominant culture. From my upbringing, I have learned that good Christian men are handsome and strong, not pretty and weak. They are tough and in control, not sensitive and dependent. Men eventually marry a woman, and do not prefer to be with men. They punch, hit, and wrestle for fun (as in sports), and don't make flower arrangements or simply visit.

Yet all these messages are so one-sided that they gave me

an unhealthy self-definition as a male. Our church and society still promote the notion that a *real* man does not act like a woman or appear to be a sissy. They condition us to think that a man should not appear soft, effeminate, or weak. But this is an inadequate portrayal of women and of refined men, and it is unduly limiting for men everywhere. Everyone has strengths; everyone has limitations.

A few years ago my friends and I decided to have a different kind of party on October 31. We decided to have a Halloween party where everyone was to come dressed as a person of the opposite sex. We called it the "Gender Bender Halloween Bash." We had a lot of fun. Wanting to portray a stereotypical Mennonite mother, I shaved my legs, stuffed balloons down my dress, and put a wig on my head.

After the night was over, I made some observations. Whereas most women felt okay with their new gender roles, many of the men were visibly nervous, embarrassed, or uncomfortable. One man covered himself up as he ran from his car to the safety of the interior of our home. Another man failed to dress up at all, saying, "I don't do that."

It was funny to see a man dressed as a woman. I think part of it was the oddness that made it funny—like wearing underwear on your head or putting sunglasses on a dog. But at another level, I found our laughter that evening quite disturbing. I felt as if every time we laughed at men dressed up as women, it did two things: It was belittling for women, and it reinforced the unhealthy, tough-guy stereotype for us men.

In trying to act like a man and not like a woman, I have stifled some of my body's reactions. For example, I don't know how to cry very well. I wish I could weep, shed some tears, be really sad, and let out some emotions when I go through pain, loss, or tragedy. Instead, I just sit there thinking, "Right now, I should be sadder." I remember one time I went to a retreat center with a less-inhibited friend. He ran across the open field and lifted his arms as if he was flying (he was!). I felt my body groan under self-restraint. I wanted to dance around and celebrate the goodness of life and creation, but I couldn't do it. Instead, I sat down and wrote about it in my journal.

Another example is my reaction to pain. If I accidentally stub my toe or pinch my finger, I might yell or curse, but I will not cry or whimper, which seems like the natural and most appropriate response. In this way, I feel a little dead to what's happening to my body. In trying to act like a man, I have somehow stifled my body's grief mechanism. I'm more prone to lash out than shed a tear. I'd like that to change, and I'd like the church to help that change.

My Body and the Bible

When I think of the Bible and my body, I have likely been influenced most by Paul's teachings on the flesh and the spirit. For example, Paul says, "To set the mind on the flesh is death, but to set the mind on the Spirit is life and peace. For this reason the mind that is set on the flesh is hostile to God; it does not submit to God's law—indeed it cannot, and those who are in the flesh cannot please God" (Rom. 8: 6-8).

I wanted to please God. Therefore, I thought I had to conquer the flesh by suppressing my bodily desires for food, sex, rest, and activity. I had to "mortify my flesh." Even Jesus said to the tempter in the desert, "One does not live by bread alone" (Luke 4:4). I took that to mean I should starve myself to get closer to God.

Again, I think one-sidedness can be damaging. I have sought a balance between my body and my spirit. They are not as separate as I used to think. God created me in this body. Paul says, "You are God's temple" (1 Cor. 3:16). I take this to mean that we should love and care for our bodies.

I hope the church can take a wholistic approach to body issues for men and women. I hope we can accept people who are big and small, tall and short, muscular and tender, and spiritual and physical. I hope we can blur the lines between what is masculine and feminine, and value everyone, made in the image of God.

Conclusion

We both had difficult times accepting and living with our bodies. Our journeys to self-acceptance could have been easier if our community had been more open about body issues and unhelpful gender stereotypes. Here are some suggestions we have for church communities wishing to address these issues:

• Adults can talk more openly about what happens to our bodies and thereby encourage younger people to talk. For example, we can be more open about things such as miscarriage, inability to conceive, menopause, prostate cancer, and breast cancer.

• Sunday school classes for adults and youth can examine the influence of popular culture on our concepts of beauty, love, sex, masculinity, and femininity.

• Churches can hold events, celebrations, and parties for children as they mature. For example, one Mennonite church held a party for all their 13-year-olds—to celebrate their age and acknowledge the changes in their bodies.

• Special courses, workshops, or retreats can be offered for church members to explore body-image issues. They can be in separate groups, for men only, and for women only, addressing topics such as cultural influences on our physical identity, biblical views of the body, stories of pain and recovery, creative movement, examining gender stereotypes, and experiencing God with our senses.

What Do You Think?

(Due to the sensitive nature of some questions, discussion may be easier in separate groups: *for women*, and *for men*.)

1. What messages do you see your church or culture telling you about how to be a man or woman? How have these messages affected the way you view and feel about your body?

2. *For women:* How does your perception of your body differ from your mother's perception of her body?

3. *For men:* How does your perception of your body differ from your father's perception of his body?

4. How well does the following statement reflect your experience? "I feel a little dead to what's happening to my body." Explain, as you feel comfortable.

5. How can the church help to change how men and women experience their bodies?

6. Do you agree or disagree with this statement? "I hope we can blur the lines between what is masculine and feminine." Why? Why not?

If You Want to Read More

Human Sexuality in the Christian Life. General Conference Mennonite Church and Mennonite Church, 1985.

May, Melanie. *A Body Knows.* Continuum Pub. Co., 1995.

Nelson, James. *Embodiment: An Approach to Sexuality and Christian Theology.* Augsburg, 1978.

Nelson, James B. *The Intimate Connection: Male Sexuality, Masculine Spirituality.* Westminster, 1988.

6

Physical and Sexual Abuse:
Violence in Gender Relationships

Carol Penner

Carol Penner lives in Vineland, Ontario, with her husband, Eugene. She spends most of her time caring for their two children, Katie and Alex. She works part-time for MCC Ontario in the area of domestic violence, and has a doctoral thesis in progress. She edited this book.

THERE WAS a time when I saw sexual harassment, wife battering, sexual abuse, and rape as social problems that happened to people somewhere *out there*. I was concerned and horrified as I listened to the news and read the statistics, but the perceived distance between me and the problems made me feel safe. The veneer of safety is now gone. Why? All because of different one-on-one conversations over the past number of years.

I heard troubling words spoken by some of my closest friends and even members of my family. "He used to hit me when he was angry." "She'd beat me with whatever was nearest—a belt, an electrical cord, her hand." "For years my father abused me." They shared their stories when they were able to bear sharing it, and when I could be trusted to hear. I have come to see that survivors and perpetrators are people I know and love.

Violence pervades many human relations. This is a fact. People do degrade, enslave, murder, rob, rape, and oppress each other. The relationships between people of different skin color, religion, nationality, and class have all been marked by violence.

In this chapter I want to look at the way relationships between men and women are marked by violence. I want to do this in the context of our Christian faith. What does it mean to be women and men in the church? How do we respond to violence when it does happen? How do we work to prevent it?

Violence and Gender

Physical violence can take many forms. Someone can push, punch, hit, or slap you. They can choke you, tie you up, or hurt you with a weapon. They can bite or kick or burn you, pull your hair, or throw things at you. This is just a partial list.

Sexual violence can also take many forms. Someone can overpower you, threaten you, or hurt you, to engage in sexual contact. This may include fondling, kissing, or vaginal, oral, or anal rape. It may involve forcing you to look at sexual acts or sexually explicit material.

Emotional violence is another form of oppression more difficult to document or describe. Yet its effects can leave scars that are difficult to heal. In this chapter I am focusing on physical and sexual violence, although any type of violence which degrades another person is a sin.

In our society, men are more likely to be perpetrators and women to be victims of sexual and physical violence. This is not to say that men cannot be victims, and that women cannot be perpetrators. However, the usual violence between genders is male aggression against women.

In 1993, the government agency Statistics Canada surveyed 12,300 women. The results showed that 39 percent of the women had been sexually assaulted by a man. Measures of violence for the survey were restricted to Canadian Criminal Code definitions of sexual assault. For those women who had been married or lived with a man, 29 percent had been physically or sexually assaulted by their partner at some point during the relationship. Fully one-third of the women assaulted by their partners feared for their lives at some point during the abusive relationship (Juristat Service Bulletin; see list below).

Men are also abused by women, but it happens less often, as statistics show. Violence of any sort, whether perpetrated by men or women, must be condemned. Yet one gender is far more often the perpetrator. This fact calls for a closer look.

Here the church is indebted to the women's movement. Feminist theorists have explored the connection between violence against women and women's status in society. They have documented the systemic domination of men over women through time. They have drawn the connections between violence against women and women's lack of political voice and low economic status in society.

Women have gained political strength and representation. Only in that way has violence against women been taken seriously. This has meant a change in the criminal code. For example, rape is now defined more broadly than vaginal penetration, and it is now a crime for a man to rape his wife. The women's movement has called for an end to discrimination against women on the basis of their gender.

The Mennonite church has historically had an uneasy

relationship with the feminist movement. Their reforms have often collided with values the church has held. In the last century, feminists campaigned for clothing reform (to provide less-cumbersome and more-practical dress for women), birth control, votes for women, and education and employment opportunities. All these proposals have been vilified at some point or another by the church. These reforms were all eventually accepted by most sectors of the Christian church as good and positive changes.

Yet the Mennonite church has had reason, along with the rest of the Christian tradition, to be wary of the feminist movement. It challenges some of the church's most deeply held beliefs. Christianity has historically claimed that men are spiritually ordained to be leaders over women. This belief can still be practically observed in a variety of churches, from the male system of priest-bishops-popes of the Catholic church, to the all-male church councils of certain Protestant denominations.

While male dominance is easily seen on an institutional level, it is also present on a personal scale, where churches teach women to be subject to their husbands. Feminist theologians have critiqued this patriarchal part of the Christian tradition. They cite biblical teachings that God created male and female equal. They claim that unequal relationships between men and women were a consequence of the Fall and not ordained of God. Some denominations have adopted this feminist viewpoint as consistent with the Christian tradition, and have denounced the historical oppression of women. Others have rejected the feminist viewpoint as unsound.

In the Mennonite church, there are differences of opinion. At the 1993 Mennonite Church Assembly in Philadelphia, this difference was evident in discussions around a document about male violence against women. Some representatives believed that patriarchy should be denounced; others felt that patriarchy was divinely ordained.

The 1993 resolution was passed by putting the discussion of patriarchy into a preamble. The document then begins by stating that there was difference among the assembled delegates over the biblical interpretation expressed in the preamble. Significantly, all of the delegates could agree that male violence against women should be denounced.

Not in My Church!

The statistics I've quoted and the discussion of patriarchy may leave some readers uncomfortable. Men may be uncomfortable because they feel guilt by association or may feel they are unfairly lumped together in the same gender with people who commit these crimes. Women may be reminded of the precariousness of their safety. Both groups may want to disbelieve the statistics.

You may find the statistics unbelievable because you feel they don't represent your circle of family and friends. I remember one man in my church publicly declaring, "I can't believe that sort of thing happens in our Mennonite churches." I knew several stories of violence against women in our congregation. No doubt he was not aware of them. His public statement made it unlikely that anyone would confide in him.

There are many reasons why people keep stories of abuse private. Perpetrators obviously don't want their actions to be known. They would have to be accountable for how they have hurt and betrayed others.

Survivors are often afraid of the vulnerability they show when they tell a story of abuse. It is hard to find words to describe something too painful for words. Some survivors fear they will not be believed, or that they will be blamed for causing the abuse. Some don't share their stories because they've buried it deep inside. Talking about it would bring back memories they don't want to think about. Others remain in abusive relationships and fear reprisal if they tell.

Gender adds another layer to these reasons for not

telling. A friend confided to me what happened when she told her mother and sister that her husband was physically abusing her. They responded, "What did you do to make him so angry? Why can't you be a better wife?" There are societal expectations that women will be the caregivers and smooth things over. If things break down, they are blamed.

Similarly, there are societal expectations for men. How can a man admit he was sexually abused as a teenager when men are supposed to be tough and unemotional? It would mean admitting that men, too, are vulnerable and can be hurt deeply.

How can a young woman in the church believably accuse her senior pastor of molesting her, when there were no witnesses and everyone respects the pastor as an upright man? She would likely be accused of fabricating the story just to get attention. The pastor's authority because of his office and his age is reinforced by his gender, making him the believable one in the eyes of the church.

Similar combinations of gender with race or economic status make it difficult for survivors to successfully confront people who have abused them. It is understandable that so many survivors remain silent.

The Church Divided

In spite of the fact that so many people have experienced sexual and physical violence, it is a sad fact that many congregations have never openly discussed these issues. Some congregations look at abuse only when confronted with a particular case within their own congregation. This can be traumatic not only for the survivor, but for the whole congregation.

The revelation that someone is a perpetrator is usually met with disbelief and shock, especially if the person is a well-respected and active member in the church. Some people may rally around the perpetrator and denounce the accusations and those making allegations. Others minimize or dismiss the abuse as a minor misdemeanor. A perpetrator may feel some superficial emotional or political support. Yet it may be difficult for leaders to find church members who will walk with perpetrators on the long road through denial to repentance, confession, and restitution.

Those people who believe the survivor and acknowledge the severity of the abuse are likely to be profoundly shaken. They must come to terms with the fact that a perpetrator of abuse is not a shadowy someone in the newspaper, but a friend, a family member, a brother or sister in Christ. They must acknowledge the sense of betrayal they feel that someone whom they loved and trusted was capable of terrible evil. They often become suspicious of their own ability to judge others.

Believing the victim-survivor will involve walking with someone who is experiencing intense feelings of hurt, anger, or rage over long periods of time. Some people are supportive initially, but soon tire of the emotional energy needed for support and wish that the survivor would "get over it."

The survivor can feel left out as the congregation bickers over how to talk about the abuse. Discussions may center immediately around forgiveness rather than accountability. Survivors may feel that the church is unwilling to hear their pain. Since the majority of survivors are female, there is a tendency to dismiss them as being "overly emotional," rather than acknowledging the depth of the trauma.

Following Jesus

It is a blessing that some churches make healthy responses to physical and sexual violence. Congregations have responded in healing ways to both perpetrators and survivors. I want to close with some practical suggestions to help you prepare your church to be a source of healing for survivors and perpetrators. As we do this, we'll be following Jesus.

In Matthew 25 Jesus tells his followers that every good

deed they do will be remembered on the day of judgment. The gift of a drink of cold water to the thirsty, or clothing to the naked will be remembered. Jesus' words to us in the context of physical and sexual abuse could be similar: "I was raped and you stood by me, I was battered, and you sheltered me, I was abused and you intervened" (Pellauer, xxii).

• Foster an openness about the reality of sexual and physical abuse. You can do this by encouraging your pastor to discuss abuse in sermons or in Sunday school. Have books available in your church library about this subject. Encourage leaders in your church and interested members to attend conferences on abuse and to share what they've learned with the congregation.

• Devote a Bible study series or Sunday school quarter to looking at biblical passages about physical and sexual abuse. See Melissa Miller's excellent resource (below).

• Examine your church's structure. Is there a division of labor according to gender? Does this say something about how women and men are valued in your church? Initiate discussions about patriarchal assumptions that families taught the different people in your congregation.

• Challenge two or three people in your group to familiarize themselves with resources available to both survivors and perpetrators of abuse in your community (such as counseling agencies, shelters, transition housing). Are these resources plentiful or scarce, expensive or accessible? Have them report their findings to the church.

• Consider volunteering your time in the nearest shelter for victims of abuse. Encourage your church or conference to support a voluntary service worker in one of these shelters.

• Have your congregation discuss how they could be supportive to survivors and perpetrators of abuse. This may involve a willingness to develop support or accountability groups.

What Do You Think?

(To discuss this sensitive topic, you may want to divide into groups, *for men*, *for women*. Then regather and share.)

1. Are you surprised by the statistics quoted about sexual and physical violence? Do these statistics reflect the experiences of people you know?

2. Where does your church stand on the issue of patriarchy? Is male headship ordained by God?

3. Has physical and sexual abuse ever been publicly discussed in your church? If yes, how was the discussion received? If no, can you suggest why it hasn't been discussed?

4. Has your congregation or a church you know dealt with a situation of abuse? Was it a healing or a hurtful process?

5. Discuss practical ways that your church can become a home for survivors or perpetrators of abuse who seek healing. How would your church react to a member with long-term pain, or intense emotions of rage, anger, or guilt?

If You Want to Read More

Adams, Carol J., and Marie Marshall Fortune, eds. *Violence Against Women and Children: A Christian Theological Sourcebook.* Continuum Pub. Co., 1995.

Cooper-White, Pamela. *The Cry of Tamar: Violence Against Women and the Church's Response.* Fortress, 1995.

Fortune, Marie Marshall. *Sexual Violence: The Unmentionable Sin.* Pilgrim Press, 1983.

Heggen, Carolyn Holderread. *Sexual Abuse in Christian Homes and Churches.* Herald Press, 1993.

Juristat Service Bulletin 14/7, 14/9 (Mar. 1994). Canadian Centre for Justice Statistics.

Miller, Melissa. *Family Violence: The Compassionate Church Responds.* Herald Press, 1994.

Pellauer, Mary D., Barbara Chester, and Jane Boyajian, eds. *Sexual Assault and Abuse: A Handbook for Clergy and Religious Professionals.* Harper & Row, 1987.

Poling, James Newton. *The Abuse of Power: A Theological Problem.* Abingdon, 1991.

Wilson, Earl and Sandy, Paul and Virginia Friesen, Larry and Nancy Paulson. *Restoring the Fallen: A Team Approach to Caring, Confronting, and Reconciling.* InterVarsity, 1997.

Yantzi, Mark. *Sexual Offending and Restoration.* Herald Press, 1998.

Yoder, Elizabeth G., ed. *Peace Theology and Violence Against Women.* Elkhart, Ind.: Inst. of Mennonite Studies, 1992.

7

A Black Woman's Voice

Regina Shands Stoltzfus

Regina Shands Stoltzfus lives in Cleveland, Ohio, where she was born and raised. She is married to Art Stoltzfus, and they have four children: Matthew, Danny, Rachel, and Joshua. They attend the Lee Heights Community Church. Regina works for Mennonite Conciliation Service as staff associate for urban peacemaking, and she also leads in antiracism education with the church.

LIKE MOST people, when I hear a recording of my voice, I am startled. "That's not what I sound like," I think. I am intimately acquainted with the sound of my voice—until I hear it on tape, until I hear what other people hear. Then I am often surprised. My voice has qualities unknown to me when I experience it through the same channels that others do. I wonder if the me that I think I am is the me others perceive me to be.

So it is with my Voice, the outward expression, spoken or otherwise, that I present to the world. I am an African-

American, woman, presently middle class. What do others hear? What do they see? The perception, I know, likely varies widely from the reality. If the channel is popular culture, perhaps my dark female face brings to mind the single mother on welfare, or the fast-talking urban smart aleck. Others may think of me as the strong, domineering matriarch, presiding over a gaggle of sassy children with warm but funny (and funky) wisdom. These women are not me, nor are they any other woman I know.

White women have been perceived by people of color as cold and emotionless and not to be trusted, or as naive and silly. Perhaps you are saying, "Those woman are not me, nor are they any other woman I know."

Women need to find the courage to tell each other who we are and break the silence that divides us.

We need to give voice to the truth of ourselves and the relationships lost because we have not been taught. If we fail to talk this out, we do not really believe we are God's own, that God dwells within us and moves, acts, and speaks through us.

In 1976 a book was published, *for colored girls who have considered suicide when the rainbow is enuf*. It is actually a long prose poem that eventually was produced as a play on Broadway. I still have my dog-eared copy, bought when I was seventeen and awakening to the understanding of what it meant to be black and female and living in America.

Over the years since then, I have read and reread this work, marveling at the clarity with which author Ntozake Shange expressed the joy, the pain, and the sheer craziness of living within the intersection of race, gender, and class. All of the poetry I will quote is from this book.

> somebody / anybody
> sing a black girl's song
> bring her out
> to know herself

to know you
but sing her rhythms
carin / struggle / hard times
sing her songs of life
she's been dead so long
closed in silence so long
she doesn't know the sound
of her own voice
her infinite beauty

Created in God's Image

Waiting in line at the grocery store, I gaze at the magazine display. Row after row of smiling women greet me, assuring me I can be slimmer, more organized, save money, create mouth-watering meals—be perfect. The faces selling me these dreams are overwhelmingly white, blond, blue-eyed—perfect. *They* represent the ideal American woman. I represent the *other*. We who are brown or black, with dark hair that may be nappy, are the outsiders. Still.

> In the image of God he created them; male and female he created them. God blessed them. (Gen. 1:27-28)

When I was a little girl I used to get my hair pressed with a hot metal comb by Mrs. White, the woman who lived across the street from us. My freshly washed hair was dense, thick, and incredibly nappy—what we then called bad hair. Every Saturday morning was spent sitting in Mrs. White's hot kitchen, flattening my wild hair into acceptability—into hair that would move in the wind and swing about my shoulders.

The price for this hair was staying away from moisture at all costs so that it wouldn't go back to its original state: don't get caught in rainshowers, try not to sweat, definitely don't swim. Millions of black girls grew up being prisoners to our hair. It was years before I accepted my hair in its natural state, years more before I decided I liked it. I hope my daughter, dark skinned with thick wavy hair, is able to develop a definition of beauty and worth that includes all of us, that honors all people as created in the image of God.

Of course, all women are subjected to society's definitions and restrictions about how we should look. Women of color bear an extra burden because in this country, Europeans set the standard for what is beautiful, what is feminine. An emphasis is placed on how one looks as part of determining what one is worth. Therefore, the effects can be devastating. I remember the taunts of my childhood, rhymes we black children would say to each other:

> if you're black, get back,
> if you're brown, stick around,
> if you're yellow, you're mellow,
> if you're white, you're all right

Sometimes we heard, "Act your age and not your color." These were messages absorbed from the society around us. I was aware of being black long before I was aware of any stigma associated with being female. And this perception of having race before gender persists. For example, I find that I am more distressed by depictions of Jesus as blond haired and blue eyed than I am by references to God using the male pronoun. Yet there are scores of people around me who don't understand why either should matter to me.

Choosing which issue to focus on is like deciding which of two beloved family members in crisis should be tended to first. Attention to one is seen as disloyalty to the other. In fact, people struggling against racism and sexism have long been suspicious of each other and in competition with each other. Black women have not fully moved into a societal space that is recognized by others. According to the world, women are white, blacks are men, and black women are some sort of hybrid, firmly planted neither here nor there.

However, it is important for the connections between sexism and racism to be understood if we want to work toward a vision of God's kingdom, a less-violent and more-just society. It is not enough to simply decry a generic violence. Violence against women needs to be named, and violence against people of color needs to be named. In order to name them, we need to learn to recognize them. For too long, these stories have been untold. Women's struggles must be put into a framework that includes the struggle of women of color, and antiracism work must include the voices of women.

> bein alive & bein a woman & bein colored is a metaphysical dilemma / i havent conquered yet / do you see the point
> my spirit is too ancient to understand the separation of soul and gender / my love is too delicate to have thrown back on my face

The Measure of a Woman's Life

Just after the Christmas holidays, a woman was killed in my city. She was thirty-nine years old, a nurse, a mother, a wife. Abducted from a shopping mall, her dead body was discovered a couple of days later. It was a horrible crime that made front-page news for many days, as well as being the lead story on all the local news broadcasts. The murder is yet unsolved. There are periodic human interest stories in the press about the investigation, the family's grief, and how women can keep themselves safe.

I grieve with the family of this woman because I know her life was precious and cannot be replaced, and because no person should die at the hands of another. And yet, I harbor a not-so-secret knowledge; one that seems nasty and petty to admit to in the wake of this tragedy. It is the knowledge that if this woman had been black, and especially if she had been black and poor, the story would not have been as compelling.

Another dead black woman? No big deal. It was "probably a drug deal gone bad," or "her kids are probably involved in gangs." Admitting this pains me on at least two levels. Loss of life is tragic. We are all diminished by crimes like these. A suburban wife, mother, out shopping with her kids. It could be someone I know. It could be me.

The other pain is that I am sharply reminded of the status of African-Americans when it comes to stories like this. In this country, black lives simply are not worth as much as white lives. If my regular, black life is taken, or my daughter's, my mother's, or my sister's, these deaths would not be significant losses worthy of the newspaper's front page. The community at large would not be asked to be outraged, to do something.

People who know they are not valued, tend to devalue themselves. People who do not believe their lives are sacred cannot value any life. It is easy to see why violence is destroying the lives of young black women and men.

> Do you not know that you are God's temple and that God's Spirit dwells in you? If anyone destroys God's temple, God will destroy that person. For God's temple is holy, and you are that temple. (1 Cor. 3:16-17)

The Associated Press released a story in the summer of 1995 that clearly illustrates this. That year two Kankakee, Illinois, children disappeared: a white 10-year-old boy and a black 13-year-old girl. Both children were found murdered. According to the AP article, "Christopher Meyer's case riveted the region for two weeks, prompting an extensive search and relentless news coverage. Ophelia Williams's death barely raised a cry.

"In a candid assessment, police chief William Doster said his community is simply 'numb' when it comes to black victims." If white children died from violence at the rate black children do, certainly a national emergency would be declared. Instead, it is business as usual. Black people continue to be only a symbol of what is wrong with America. To the public, violence, crime, and the (undeserving) poor all have black faces.

i usedta live in the world
really be in the world
free & sweet talking
good mornin and thank-you & nice day
uh huh
i cant now
i cant be nice to nobody
nice is such a rip-off
reglar beauty & a smile in the street
is just a set-up

i usedta be in the world
a woman in the world
i hadda right to the world
then i moved to harlem
for the set-up
a universe
six blocks of cruelty
piled up on itself
a tunnel
closin

The Meaning of Work

A well-meaning (I assume) white man once asked me what it was that convinced me to get a job. We had been talking about issues of urban life, especially poverty and crime. I consider myself to be fairly well-spoken, and think I come across as an educated, motivated person. Yet this man saw something in me which told him I had no work ethic on my own, and it was something extraordinary that caused me to seek employment.

The great divide between black women and white women has its roots in the written history of this country, beginning with slavery. Black women, children, and men put in long backbreaking hours of work for which they received no compensation. They owned nothing, not even their lives, and had no say in what work they would do.

The sexual exploitation of enslaved women did more than keep making black women into objects and nonpersons. It also gave rise to the image of white women as pure and guileless, and of black women as wanton and promiscuous. It increased the ranks of the enslaved population. It drove an unshakable wedge between two groups of women already separated by their free and captive status. It also projected onto black men the fear of cross-racial sexual aggressiveness.

In addition, the meaning of work and its centrality to the feminist movement have radically different faces for black women and for white women, stemming from this period. Black women have always "worked outside the home," often in someone else's home, raising someone else's children, while her own children fended for themselves.

During the first wave of feminist consciousness, a largely middle-class phenomenon, a chief preoccupation for white women was gaining a toehold in the workforce. Black women, and their sisters of color were already, of necessity, in the workforce, usually in low-paying jobs with little or no status, effectively rendering them even more invisible and powerless than white women.

American capitalism by necessity divides people into separate groupings according to race, sex, and class. The largest and most powerful segment is white and male. Women of color occupy the smallest and least-influential segment. Indeed, the reason this country has a *race* of people called *white* stems from the period after emancipation. At that time, the poor descendants of Europeans and Africans needed to be kept from identifying with each other on the basis of their shared poverty. If they identify together as poor, they might join forces to confront the ruling, wealthy class.

These divisions still build walls, keeping people away from each other and suspicious of others: blacks and whites, men and women, poor, working class, and middle class. Solidarity cannot be achieved by those who have always been taught that the *other* is not to be believed or trusted. The gospel proclaims something better for us to live out.

> [Christ] is our peace; in his flesh he has made both groups into one and has broken down the dividing wall, that is, the hostility between us. (Eph. 2:14)

Today, such divisions play themselves out in another scenario, the debate to "end welfare as we know it." Welfare, which wears a black face but in reality supports mostly white families, becomes important in cycles which coincide with election years. The wealthy and middle-class public, misled by politicians, cries out for welfare reform and demands poor (black) women get off the dole and work for a living. They ironically demand that these women work anywhere, even for minimum wage, without adequate childcare and with no medical insurance.

At the same time, they bemoan the fact that (white) women's foray into the workforce has been the downfall of the American family. The scenario is made even more ludicrous by the fact that welfare accounts for less than one percent of the federal budget.

Nevertheless, the church as an institution has not sought to change the things that make poor people poor. The church does not keep its own people from disparaging women, the poor, and people of color. Instead of a church-growth paradigm that separates us from those who are different, justice-seeking church folks will do well to heed the call to share resources and power with all God's people.

All who believed were together and had all things in common; they would sell their possessions and goods and distribute the proceeds to all, as any had need. Day by day, as they spent much time together in the temple, they broke bread at home and ate their food with glad and generous hearts, praising God and having the goodwill of all the people. (Acts 2:44-47)

Women and their children are the poorest people in the world. The world over, dark-skinned people are considered of less worth than people with white skin. Their cultures are not counted to be as valuable. Schools in our cities, where these poor people live, are literally falling apart, with roofs caving in, gaping holes in unpainted walls, not enough books to go around. Mass transportation neglects the neighborhoods of the people who need it the most, to reach jobs located outside the areas where they live.

These people seemingly are not worth the energy and expense of redefining the way we fund schools or distribute public services. Is the church satisfied with this? I look at my children and see the handiwork of God. May they always know that they are created in God's image. May their voices rise and combine with God's children everywhere, to make their stories known.

> i found god in myself
> & i loved her / i loved her fiercely

What Do You Think?

1. How did you feel after reading this chapter? If you felt uncomfortable, can you identify where the discomfort comes from?

2. How have you related with persons from another race? Has your experience dispelled any stereotypes you had about that group?

3. Do you think there is hope for racial reconciliation in your lifetime? Do you think the church can/should/will be a leader in this?

4. How does your race, gender, or class affect the way society treats you? How does it treat people who are different from you?

If You Want to Read More

Ayvazian, Andrea, and Beverly Daniel Tatum. "Can We Talk? It's Time for a New Conversation on Race in America." *Sojourners*, Jan.-Feb. 1996, 16-19.

Golden, Marita, and Susan Richards Shreve, eds. *Skin Deep: Black Women and White Women Write About Race.* Doubleday, 1995.

hooks, bell. *Killing Rage: Ending Racism.* Henry Holt, 1995.

Levine, Judith. "White Like Me: When Privilege Is Written on Your Skin." *Ms*, Mar.-Apr. 1994, 22-24.

Rozzell, Liane. "Double Jeopardy: Racism and Violence Against Women." In *America's Original Sin: A Study Guide on White Racism,* 25-27. *Sojourners*, 1992, expanded edition.

Shange, Ntozake. *for colored girls who have considered suicide when the rainbow is enuf.* Macmillan Pub. Co., 1977.

Wilson, Midge, and Kathy Russel. *Divided Sisters: Bridging the Gap Between Black Women and White Women.* Anchor Books, Doubleday, 1996.

8

Gender and Aging: Male or Female—What Difference Does It Make?

Katie Funk Wiebe

Katie Funk Wiebe is a prolific freelance writer and editor, and is also active as a workshop and retreat leader. She taught English for twenty-four years at Tabor College. Wiebe grew up in northern Saskatchewan, and moved to Kansas in 1962. She makes her home in Wichita.

WHEN YOU'RE old, does it make any difference whether you're male or female? Old is old, I've heard people say. Hair color is the same for older men or women. The faces of both show wrinkles. The stooped shoulders and slower walk are no respecter of gender.

Yes, men and women share certain characteristics of aging. Yet newer research reveals that men and women deal with other aspects of aging in different ways. This is the main emphasis of my chapter. Yet we must keep in mind that no two people, male or female, age exactly in the same way.

In Some Ways the Genders Age the Same
The public image of aging
Both men and women are vulnerable to the prevailing public image of aging, whatever it may be at the moment. They also experience the way society reacts to this image, rather than to them as individuals. Attitudes toward the elderly have changed over the centuries and continue to change. Elders once had a clear role in relationship with younger generations. They were respected for their knowledge, and also for their wisdom, much needed for a culture to survive. They provided the continuity between the generations necessary for a people to maintain themselves.

Today, for some people, old is old, which means being out of touch, grumpy, possibly frail and poor. It adds up to being someone who no longer has something to offer society. In filmdom and television, especially in advertisements, older adults are frequently portrayed as comical, stubborn, and foolish. The person chosen to look and act the frump invariably is an older man or woman, but more often an older woman. The butt of television advertising humor is seldom a good-looking young adult.

A more recent stereotype is of elders as wealthy, chasing the sun, looking for more and more fun and new experiences, with little sense of responsibility for anyone but themselves. After all, they did their share of work when they were younger. Older adults probably do have more discretionary income today than any other older-adult group in history. In the United States, the AARP (American Association of Retired Persons) is considered one of the most-powerful lobbies in Washington.

Sometimes there are shades of differences in these stereotypes. Men are more likely to be pictured as aging with dignity and charm, remaining attractive to younger women. When older women are the main characters in newer movies or television dramas, they may be wealthy, even sexy, much aware of who they are, and possibly domineering. Such characters depart from the older image of the older woman as lonely, frustrated, and shriveled, lacking poise, power, and personality.

The poor, elderly, black woman has four strikes against her: poverty, age, race, and gender. She seldom shows up as the main character of either television or movie scripts. More than four out of ten (44%) older black women who lived alone were poor in 1993.

Because older men and women both lack an accepted and well-defined role in church and society, they have difficulty knowing where they fit in. I have asked many groups: "What is the role of the older adult in your congregation? What does God ask of them?" I don't want to know what keeps them busy. I want to know their role, their proper and expected function in the body of Christ. These are hard questions for the church to answer today.

Physical changes

Both men and women face changes in their physical body as they grow older, changes experienced as losses. Some people say that old age is not something you die of (true), or that you are only as old as you feel. Yet increasing frailty does accompany aging.

Few people over the age of seventy-five can run a four-minute mile or race up the stairs the way they did in their youth. Gymnasts retire in their early twenties, tennis players in their thirties, and baseball players in their forties. They are aware that their physical skills are diminishing, and it is difficult to compete against younger athletes. The human body is programmed to give out by about age eighty-five.

At the risk of generalizing too much, older men may experience enlargement of the prostate gland and its accompanying woes. Women cope with decreased muscle tone of the bladder and of the muscles controlling urination. Both genders experience a decline in hormonal secretions. Men run the greater risk of heart attacks and strokes. Women suffer more from the risk of osteoporosis. In addition, both men and women may suffer from arthritis, hypertension, and hearing impairment.

The Genders Age Differently in Some Ways

Because the stories of men and women differ, their experiences with aging cannot be equated or deemed to be similar in all respects. The social class of the woman's husband has traditionally determined her status during her lifetime. Yet even if she was uneducated, according to Betty Friedan (see list below), gender transcends class in setting the quality of life in old age. Women, the largest demographic group among the elderly, do better at aging than men. What accounts for this?

The women's movement

Friedan claims that the women's movement has given women a greater sense of self-worth and control of their lives. It has brought openness about body functions, such as menstruation, menopause, and childbirth. The empty nest looks less devastating than it once did, when child-rearing was a woman's main function in life.

Experience with flexibility

At some point most older women have stopped trying to hang onto images of youthfulness. They have come to terms with their outward appearance.

Most women growing older today have had a career in addition to a background of nurturing in the home. In the work world, they have had various experiences, sometimes working full-time, sometimes part-time, sometimes dropping out for a while to look after children or even aging parents.

For men, marriage and family is often an addition to what they do vocationally, so identity issues after retirement are particularly acute for them. Women have learned greater flexibility and adaptation as they moved through other life stages. Friendships and relationships, so necessary as one ages, were usually important to women in their early decades and remain important. Some men come to late stages of life with few personal friends.

Past experience of nurturing

Older women come to aging with rich experiences in sister-hood, mentoring, caring, sorrowing with the grieving, volunteering, and so forth. These are relationships and activities some men have never developed. The volunteer world is populated mostly by women.

Demographics

Sheer demographics have given older women the edge: they far outnumber men. They are a "minority" that is a majority in their age bracket. In 1993, there were 19.5 million older women and 13.3 million older men, a sex ratio of 147 women for every 100 men. The sex ratio increased with age, ranging from 122 women to 100 men for the 65-69 group, to a high of 256 to 100 for persons 85 and older (all statistics from *Profile*).

Baby-boomer women will not subside submissively into the background the way today's older women have done. They will not let their identity or contribution be lost as experienced by women of earlier generations. I have heard researchers speak of how difficult it is to locate the given and maiden names of married women of an earlier generation.

Then a woman was often known only as Mrs. John Doe,

and her contribution if mentioned was included in the record of her husband. Why? Her contribution related to the underside of history, to use Elise Boulding's term. She maintains that this side of history is often unrecorded and unreported, because it does not relate to power, prestige, and politics.

Some gerontologists (studying aging) are convinced that because of their number and change in status in society, women will determine the quality of life in the future and influence the direction society will take.

Challenges for the Older Woman
Living alone
Older women are not without challenges, sometimes quite severe. Aloneness, often with loneliness, faces many older women. Because husbands have a lower life expectancy than women, wives are more likely to be widows with less probability for remarriage than widowers. In 1993, older men were nearly twice as likely to be married as older women: 77 percent of men, 42 percent of women. Half of all older women in 1993 were widows (48 percent). There were nearly five times as many widows (8.6 million) as widowers (1.8 million). Older women have fewer opportunities to marry and feel less freedom to invite men to marry them.

Some widows and divorcées, whose identity once was defined by a husband, may suffer guilt and discomfort in moving to a life of their own without male protection and support. On the other hand, living without a spouse challenges many widows to new learnings. It is not uncommon to hear older widows say, "After John died, I learned to . . ." The new skills include learning to drive a car, manage family finances, use a computer, and develop a new vocational skill.

Poverty
Older women are more likely to be poor. The median income of older persons in 1993 was $14,983 for males and $8,479

for females. Older women had a higher poverty rate (15 percent) than older men (8 percent).

Return to Caregiving Role

Older women are more likely to face a new crisis of caretaking for husbands, parents, and sometimes grandchildren. Mothering their own children is more or less completed. Yet older women are often seen monitoring their husband's bodies. Gail Sheehy (*New Passages*) observes that a woman carries pills in her purse that her husband must take. She even reminds him when to take them—often out of fear of becoming a widow.

Sheehy advises women to find a sense of importance and means of individual survival before children leave or husband dies. That sense of importance cannot come only from her role as worker in the home. Otherwise, she will be exposed to the very future she most dreads: depending on her husband to stay healthy and faithful to her and on her children to love her.

Parental illness may also return the woman to the nurturing role, even as it promotes the man to the senior role in the family. It is not unusual to find seventy-year-old women taking care of ninety-year-old parents and parents-in-law.

Children return to the family nest because of divorce, death, or financial hardship, with or without their children. This challenges both older men and women. Sometimes the grandchildren become the grandparents' new charge.

What About the Men?

What concerns men in retirement? According to Sheehy, often men are bothered about the degree of success they have or haven't attained in their careers. They miss the people they worked with (as do women). Men miss working toward a goal. They fear losing sexual potency. They have to face the memory that they were absent or poor fathers in their earlier years. Yet mentally healthy men continue to find excitement in life, take pleasure in their offspring, and look for new challenges.

Men are more likely to enter the last period of life with a spouse, with a home they own (85 percent compared to 67 percent for women), and with more financial assets than women. Labor force participation for the older man is about 16 percent compared to 8 percent for women.

Identity

Men who have been achievement oriented, who did not allow emotions to surface while in their formative and working years, will struggle more with identity than women. At retirement, they face big changes in loss of power, control, and dominance, affecting their self-esteem. For men, the task after retirement is to find a new identity. This is a task more women will face as they too continue in careers until the end of their working lives. In the future, it may also be harder for highly motivated women careerists to form new friendships once they leave the work world.

The loss of identity at retirement may lead to despondency and suicide, writes Dwight Roth (in *Life After Fifty*). While older adults represent about 12 percent of the U.S. population, they comprise 25 percent of the people who take their own lives, according to Charles Zastrow. "The highest rate of suicide within the elderly as a group is among white males, for whom retiring from a prestigious career is a crucial change" (Roth).

Women are more likely to have been practicing withdrawal and reentry all their lives. They have therefore developed greater resilience to change. Women have generally allowed themselves greater freedom to grow, especially through reading and group interaction. Note the numerous women's study and fellowship groups.

Remaining involved in a long series of lessening involvements as one ages is more likely to be a man's privilege than a woman's. *Climbing Down the Ladder* by Linden Wenger, former teacher and pastor, is not likely the story a woman could write about remunerated church work. Women are not eased out of church work as many male church workers are, slowly being given less and less responsibility.

Widowerhood

Older men are more likely to have a spouse to lean on than are older women. But they are more likely to be devastated by the loss of a spouse. Sheehy writes that older men without wives are more vulnerable to depression than widowed or divorced women. That depression may lead to deterioration of physical health. She quotes a Methodist church deacon as saying that he sees many of his male parishioners in their sixties spending more and more time at home. "They start slipping into a spiritual and social isolation." Men are more likely than women to follow their wives into the grave during the first six months to a year after they are alone.

"The comfort of mature love" is the single thing that most determines "older men's outlook on life," Sheehy writes, based on extensive research.

Does the Bible Offer Any Help?

The Bible says little specifically about gender and aging. Yet inherent on its pages is the staunch belief that both older men and women deserve respect for their wisdom and goodness, a standard practice of ancient cultures.

Both men and women are invited to service. God uses young and old in the work of serving the kingdom of God. The psalmist sang about the righteous: "In old age they still produce fruit; they are always green and full of sap, showing that the Lord is upright; he is my rock" (Ps. 92:14). A prime example is the aging Caleb. When the Promised Land was being divided, he asked Joshua to give him the hill country that Moses had promised him (Josh. 14:12). He wanted to die climbing.

In 1 Timothy 5:1-20, Paul writes at length to the younger Timothy on how to treat older men and women. The church is a family. When members are unequal in age, the older men and women are to be treated as parents. Yet age does not make admonition unnecessary. To the end, older people remain human. They are still on a journey of faith, susceptible of falling into sin, but also able to receive renewed measures of God's grace.

This in itself is probably one of the greatest truths we can learn from Scripture about older men and women. They are still pilgrims on the way to glory. They can still grow, change, reach, hope, dream, even as they can stumble and fall. They remain human and in danger of sinning, and therefore in need of God's grace and forgiveness until their death. That truth should direct the church's ministry to its older men and women.

However, older men and women also have responsibilities. Titus 2:1-5 is one of few passages that speak to both older men and women. Older men are to be temperate in thought, word, and act. In other words, they are to act dignified to be worthy of respect. They are to be self-controlled and strong in faith, love, and endurance.

In biblical times, older women were often the object of ridicule in Greek comedies and accused of spreading old wives' tales. The apostle Paul therefore admonishes them to be reverent in their demeanor, not slanderers or gossipers. They were not to be addicted to wine, but to teach what is good to young women.

Paul recognized that older widows might be lonely and needy. Therefore, the church should provide for them. Respect for widows over sixty was to be based on the way they had conducted themselves when younger. They had brought up children, practiced hospitality, washed the feet of saints, helped those in trouble, and generally devoted themselves to good deeds.

The role of older men and women is changing, as is the role of other men and women. Recent studies show men just now discovering that the essence of masculinity is not unchanging. Women discovered that several decades ago. Now older men and women have the task of discovering together that God has given them roles they eventually will have let go of, by default. God has imbedded human limitations in this good Creation.

As I say in *Older Adults and Faith*, it is important for young and old to learn anew that "all of life is sacred from the embryo in the womb to the older adult on his or her deathbed." All are needed in the work of the kingdom.

What Do You Think?

1. Assign each class member the task of watching for stereotypes of older adults on television this week, especially in commercials. What did you discover? Do you like what you discovered?

2. Do you agree that men and women deal with old age in different ways? Why? Why not?

3. Invite some older women who live alone to share with you their experiences of aging.

4. Some men and women have received their identity mostly from their career. What can help them adjust to life without a vocational identity?

5. What do you see as the role of older men and women in your congregation? How can the church help change the public image of the older adult?

If You Want to Read More

Cole, Thomas R. *The Journey of Life: A Cultural History of Aging in America.* Cambridge Univ. Press, 1992.
Friedan, Betty. *The Fountain of Age.* Simon & Shuster, 1993.

Profile of Older Americans 1994. American
    Association of Retired Persons.

Roth, Dwight. In *Life After Fifty* (see under Wiebe).

Sheehy, Gail. *New Passages: Mapping Your Life Across
    Time.* Random House, 1995.

Welch, Elizabeth. *Learning to Be 85.* Upper Room Books,
    1991.

Wenger, Linden M. *Climbing Down the Ladder: A Teacher
    and Pastor Reflects on His Retirement.* Good Books,
    1993.

Wiebe, Katie Funk. *Border Crossing: A Spiritual Journey.*
    Herald Press, 1995.

_____, ed. *Life After Fifty: A Positive Look at Aging in the
    Faith Community.* Faith & Life, 1993.

_____. *Older Adults and Faith: Making New Maps.* Faith
    & Life, 1995.

_____. *Prayers of an Omega: Facing the Transitions of
    Aging.* Herald Press, 1994.

9

The Church Is Not Noah's Ark:
Singleness in the Church

Miles Zimmerly Wiederkehr

Miles Zimmerly Wiederkehr is a former soybean breeder, seminary student, single person, and community development worker from Ohio, Bangladesh, Indiana, and Saskatchewan. He is now living in Ontario with his wife, Ruth Isaac Wiederkehr. They worship with the Welcome Inn in Hamilton.

AS I WRITE this, it is near Christmastime, certainly a family time of year. Yet for many people, it is a lonely time of year. It might have been lonely for me, for I am the only one of my birth family in North America. But this Christmas is busy, not lonely. I am drawn into my wife's extended family. It's good to be married.

Also as I write this, I am in a time of transition, between

jobs. Being married really complicates my decision-making about job and vocation. It would be good to be single!

Consider

• In our recently adopted confession of faith, we say, "We hold that within the church family, the goodness of being either single or married is honored. Equal importance is given to persons who belong to nuclear families, to those in extended families, and to persons who are single."

• Paul says, in essence, "The one who marries does well, and the one who refrains from marriage will do better" (1 Cor. 7:38).

• Our practice is such that competent single women in their seventies are called "the Janzen girls."

What do we really believe about singleness?

Marriage and the People of God

Let's begin by taking a look at what the Bible says about singleness. When we do, we quickly find that the Bible is not a single book, but a collection of books written over hundreds of years. The Bible has many things to say about marriage and singleness, and the different voices don't always agree.

In the first place, my pun about a *single* book is not simply a poor attempt at humor. The Bible has many voices: it was written and compiled by a community of faith, and it is read and interpreted by that same community, the people of God. We believe that both the writing and the interpreting are led by God's Spirit. So togetherness is built in, by God's design. God created Adam and Eve and ordained marriage. Thus Adam and Eve also participated in the creation of this people of God by being fruitful and multiplying (Gen. 1–2).

The story of Noah loading his ark two-by-two is the story of a new creation by procreation (Gen. 6:11-22). Marriage and children are expected for the people of God in the Old Testament. Even the symbol of joining the people is associated with birth: circumcision of baby boys on the eighth day (Gen. 17). Among the people of the covenant, there is an emphasis on families.

In the New Testament, things are new. The people of God are still chosen, and there is a stronger emphasis on individuals choosing. The people are joined not through birth but through rebirth, birth from above (John 3:3, 5). Now the symbol of joining is not circumcision but baptism. This baptismal sign is not just for Jewish males, but for everyone who decides to die with Jesus and to be reborn into a new life in Jesus.

Paul works within this new situation when he suggests that marriage is good, but singleness is better (1 Cor. 7:25-40). In the new reality, and with the end near, Paul asserts that a continuing earthly society is less important than being as free as possible to work for the kingdom of heaven, which is breaking in all around.

The story of the Ethiopian eunuch (Acts 8:26-40) is a wonderful example of how this can be good news. The eunuch was returning from a pilgrimage to Jerusalem, where he would have been excluded from the assembly (Deut. 23:1). There was so much that attracted him to belief in the God of Abraham, Isaac, and Jacob! And yet he could not take his place in that patriarchal family. As he went, he was puzzling over the (Old Testament) Scriptures. Not just any text, but one about eunuchs being included (Isa. 53:7-12; 56:3-5). So he was ripe for Philip's good news that God is also the God of Jesus and other suffering servants who are single and childless.

At the same time, we have the stories of Cornelius (Acts 10) and the jailer (Acts 16) being baptized with their whole households. Timothy came from a Christian family (2 Tim. 1:5). Human families and marriage continued within the New Testament people of God. But they were not the basis of peoplehood. The new covenant in Christ bound believers together (1 Cor. 11:23-26).

A Brief History of Singleness in the Church

As the church lived on through the centuries, there came a shift from the idea that "the one who marries does well" to the idea that "marriage is not as bad as the alternative: unbridled immorality." Christians tended to see sex as sinful, and marriage as a limit on sin. Priests were to hold to a higher standard and be celibate.

By the 1500s, however, the institution of the celibate priesthood was full of hypocrisy. Many priests and even popes openly kept mistresses and had children. Obbe Philips, the man who ordained Menno Simons, was the son of a priest. One of the main protest actions of the Reformation was the marriage of priests, nuns, and monks. Examples are Martin Luther, and among the Anabaptists, Menno Simons, Michael Sattler and his wife Margaretha, Melchior Hoffmann, Leonhard Schiemer, Dirk Philips, and Balthasar Hubmaier. These all left their vows and married.

So at the time of the first Anabaptists, it was important to affirm that marriage was good. For the early, persecuted generations of Anabaptists, however, it was still quite clear that commitment to God came before commitment to spouse and family. Such believers were willing to die and entrust their families to the care of God. Marriage was good, though not as important as being a faithful disciple.

However, Mennonites later became the "quiet in the land," the pendulum swung further, and marriage came to be seen as almost the only acceptable state for adults.

And Now?

How are singles treated in the Mennonite church today? At least at times, not very well. All too often the church believes it is Noah's ark, and everything proceeds two-by-two.

This can mean that the single person is left out. One time two of us were setting the table for a dinner party. After we had finished, I realized that we were short one place, so I added one. I came back to find my friend taking it off again: "We don't need it." I tactfully started naming people. When I came to our single guest, my friend said, "Oh, of course. I just counted the five couples." How does it feel if we always count by twos and leave no room at the table for single people?

Singles may also feel second class in the church, or not fully adult. For instance, in one church the only way to get out of the post-high Sunday school class is to marry. Again, I recently heard a woman tell a warm and wonderful story of her wedding day. Then she described some of her fears of marriage: "I knew I was leaving girlhood behind forever." What would that comment mean to a single woman her age?

At times single people may also feel that they are seen only as objects for marriage. This experience may feel like being treated as sick persons needing care until they're well (married). "How are you? Any special friends we should know about? No? Oh, that's too bad." This line of questioning may fit with a single person's experience, but it may just as likely not. And even if the single would rather be married, focusing on marital status misses an awful lot of the whole person.

The analogy of sickness may be stretched further in that the concern for the *patient* may be mingled with fear of the *disease*. The concerned question subtly points out that the single person is *sick* and needs to be *cured* (get married), and communicates a fear for the questioner's own safety. How would this message affect you over a lifetime?

Think for a moment of a single person in the church, one whom you admire. Now compare notes. My guess is that most of you have thought of a single woman. Not only is this based on my own experience, but also on statistics. Kauffman and Harder, in their survey of Mennonite and Brethren in Christ church members in 1972, found that among those 45 years and over, 9.3 percent of the women never married, compared to only 1.6 percent of the men (176; see list below).

After demographic changes to 1989 are factored in,

there was no evidence of change in the proportion of people who never marry (Kauffman and Driedger, 111-112). I believe that there has been a special place in the church for single women, but no secure place for single men.

Single women have done much of the mission work of the church. They found greater freedom on the mission field than in their home communities. They also found a place through the institution of the deaconess, a committed sisterhood of nurses begun in Germany and Russia and continued until recently in the General Conference in North America. In general, a woman was free for "church work" only if she didn't marry. A man was freed up by marrying, almost as if a man had to be married to work for the church. Why this difference?

I believe this difference in our view of single women and single men is due to our belief about men and women in general. One relevant myth is the unquenchable male sex drive. Men cannot deny their sexuality (presumably women can), and so the bachelor is perceived to be under a cloud of temptation. Think of the difference in connotation of *bachelor* and *old maid.*

A second myth is that the man is necessarily the pursuer and initiator in courtship. The single man can always ask and so has really chosen to be single, while the single woman can (customarily) only wait to be asked. Therefore, an unmarried man is viewed with some suspicion, while an unmarried woman is viewed with pity.

Third, in terms of traditional gender roles, men need marriage more than women do. Specifically, as mentioned above, they need marriage as a sexual outlet. Additionally, we tend to think of men as having few intimate friends other than their wives, and as being helpless around the house. Women are seen as fine in those areas, but as needing social and financial security—an income and a protector. These things they were sometimes able to get from church work.

All this means that traditionally a woman could, to some

extent, choose between two viable but imperfect or unsatis-
factory options. A man might be able to "have it all," both
marriage and serving the church. Or he might end up with
nothing. To some extent, he was not completely free to
choose. Single people in the church today are challenging
those stereotypes.

What We Can Learn from Singleness

We can learn about *being alone* and *being together*. Mary Mae
Schwartzendruber writes, "Our individuality always makes us
single persons even if we are not all unmarried" (8). At the
same time, we are all created to relate, to be together. All
humans share needs which are met in relationship. These
needs may be met in marriage or in singleness. Either state
may be freeing or binding. Either state may be committed or
irresponsible. In either state we may find wholeness and longing. In either state we may find relationship or loneliness.

We can learn about *intimacy* and *sexual intercourse*.
Intimacy is "the experience of a sustained close familiarity
with another's life; it is to know another person from the
inside" (Harold Bauman, in *Human Sexuality*, 55). Both singles
and marrieds can know intimacy, including physical intimacy.
Sexual intercourse is only one kind of physical intimacy, and
we affirm it as a gift of God in marriage. Yet healthy celibate
singleness shows the possibility of wholeness, relationship,
and intimacy without sexual intercourse. This is a helpful
reminder in our cultural context.

We can learn about *Christian vocation*. While it might be
easy to say, "Either singleness or marriage is fine," what are we
to make of the teachings of Jesus and Paul? (Matt. 19:10-12;
1 Cor. 7). In some sense, singleness is better. In saying that, I
look at singleness as a gift (1 Cor. 7:7). I acknowledge marriage as a norm, then, in a sense; but singleness goes beyond
the normal. Calling singleness a *gift* makes a claim that it is
beyond our doing, that faithful singleness comes from God.

Thus, singleness is not to be envied or pitied, but accepted for the building up of Christ's body, the church.

Different gifts are given for tasks which differ in type and degree. Many of us are uncomfortable with these differences. We tend to assume that since we are all equal before God, we should all be identical. If we say that someone is unmarried for the sake of the kingdom, then we may conclude that that person must be trying to be spiritually superior. Their singleness is hard to accept. We tend to feel that there must be one right way of doing and being—like me! Yet if singleness is a gift from God, don't we need to honor it as such?

Marrieds have tensions if they think singles are questioning the value of things to which married couples have committed their lives. If a married person's identity is solely in marriage, children, house, possessions, sexual activity—then it may be taken as an affront if a single person is just as happy without all that. If a single person's identity is solely in church work or a simple life—then it may be taken as an affront to say that one can also serve God in raising a middle-class Christian family. Can we learn to accept each other?

What might be the nature of this vocation, this gift, of singleness? A sign of it will be a motivation of love, not fear. All too often marriage is from fear of aloneness. Singleness may also be from fear, fear of the other gender, of marriage and sex, of commitment. Yet the gift of singleness is not negative, but a commitment to a positive good, a commitment of love.

I think sometimes the vocation of singleness will be for a certain work, in other cases for a priority on freedom to do what needs doing. This vocation is in the context of all believers placing the highest priority on our relationship with God, and on seeking God's kingdom first of all (Matt. 6:33; 10:37-39). Still, the single person may have more freedom to serve in demanding roles, or in service settings of great risk or isolation.

Changes in Singleness

Our society is changing. As a result, we are confronted more and more with singles, whom we had formerly been able to overlook.

• There are more singles than ever in society at large (42% of U.S. adults in 1993 Census Bureau figures, 38% of Canadian adults in 1993 Statistics Canada figures).

• People are marrying later in life. From 1975 to 1991 in Canada, the average age at first marriage rose from 22.0 to 25.7 for women and from 24.4 to 27.7 for men. While the myth of romantic fulfillment still looms large, the expectation· of marriage as a rite of passage is lessening.

• The extended family is declining in importance. This both eliminates some of the former family structure of which singles were a part. It opens opportunities for participation in new relationship structures not based on kinship.

• People don't stay married. While we have been talking mostly of the never married, there are also large numbers of singles-again. This is partly due to a soaring divorce rate, but also to an increase in some people far outliving their spouses, due in turn to longer life and less pressure to remarry.

With these shifts in our society, our assumptions and beliefs are also changing. We are tending to discard an earlier assumption that a man or a woman is a part of a whole which can only be completed in marriage. In this changed context, a movement for the wider acceptance of singles in the church has begun. In the past twenty years, Mennonite authors have been dealing with singleness as a practical way of living a Christian life, rather than as an acceptable alternative to the *norm* of marriage.

What Can We Do?

Our 1995 Mennonite Confession of Faith speaks of the church family. I wish we could grow toward that! Instead, many see the church as a product to be consumed rather than a caring home, "the place where, when you have to go there, they have to take you in" (Robert Frost, "Death of the Hired Man"). There needs to be room for everyone.

In other words, I am not talking about some warm fuzzy sense of family, for which you shop around from church to church. I am talking about the practical reality of a church where we are all family, and where we make it work because, no matter what, we are brothers and sisters. In such a church, both singles and marrieds are full members. We share as peers. We share in parenting. Perhaps we share our living space. Voluntary Service households are examples of Christian households not centered on marriage.

A second and perhaps simpler action is to dream together of an alternative to a wedding as a rite of passage to adulthood. The wedding ritual is important: it marks a change of status, it calls forth the commitment of the community, and it helps practically in setting up a household. For a committed single, those same things need to happen—but there is no rite for it. Let's come up with one! Perhaps housewarming events, or commissioning to service. Maybe we should regard baptism as the prime rite of passage for every believer.

Third, but basic to all we attempt, let's listen to one another. Stereotypes kill relationships with real people. To know real people, we must listen to their unique stories. The widowed person, the divorced person, the person committed to singleness, the single person wanting to be married—each has a different story.

What Do You Think?

1. Are single men and single women treated differently in the church? If so, why does this happen?

2. In your church family, think of single persons you have known. How did singleness work for them? against them?

3. In your church family, think of married persons you

have known. How did marriage work for them? against them? What is your experience of singleness or marriage?

4. What unique gifts can single people offer the church? What unique gifts can the church offer single people?

5. Read 1 Corinthians 7:25-40. Is it possible for a married person to be as wholeheartedly dedicated to God as a single person?

6. Read Matthew 19:12. Becoming "eunuchs for the sake of the kingdom of heaven" points to a radically different set of priorities, not putting hope even in that which is common to all human cultures; our children. Are these our priorities?

If you want to read more

Burkholder, Myrna. "Singleness." In *The Mennonite Encyclopedia*, 5:828-829. Herald Press, 1990.

Human Sexuality in the Christian Life. 1985 statement by General Conference Mennonite Church and Mennonite Church. Herald Press, Congregational Publishing, 1986.

Kauffman, J. H., and Leland Harder. *Anabaptists Four Centuries Later.* Herald Press, 1975.

_____ and Leo Driedger. *The Mennonite Mosaic: Identity and Modernization.* Herald Press, 1991.

Schwartzendruber, Mary Mae. "Being Single." In *Being Brothers and Sisters: Stories of Personal Need in the Church.* Ed. Diana Brandt. Faith & Life Press, 1984.

Yoder, Bruce, and Imo Jeanne Yoder, eds. *Single Voices.* Herald Press, 1982.

Magazines with interesting articles about singleness:
Gospel Herald, July 13, 1993.
Mission Focus 19/1 (Mar. 1991).
Mennonite Central Committee Women's Concerns Report: "Single Women." Mar.-Apr. 1994.
"Embracing Change: Women at Midlife." May-June 1996.

10

Mothering and Fathering: The Change in Us

Wes Bergen and Carol Penner

Wes Bergen is a stay-at-home father of two children, one and four years old. Originally from Saskatchewan, Wes and his wife, Deborah, live in North Newton, Kansas. Wes is part-time teaching minister at New Creation Fellowship Church. Carol Penner and her husband, Eugene, live in Vineland, Ontario. Carol spends most of her time caring for their two children, Katie and Alex. She works part-time for MCC Ontario in the area of domestic violence, has a doctoral thesis in progress, and edited this book. Wes and Carol have been friends for many years and were living in the same town when this chapter was written.

IF YOU become a parent, you may find yourself changing in ways that you did not anticipate. How will these changes affect your understanding of God and the way you live out your Christian faith? Will these changes be different if you are a man or if you are a woman? What experiences are common to both fathers and mothers?

In this chapter we address these questions by reflecting on what parenting has meant to us. We each have two children in our respective families. Both of us have been stay-at-home parents. Our stories reflect our own contexts. We are aware that our experiences might be different from parents who work full-time outside the home, or who have older or grown-up children. We hope our stories will invite you to think about and share your own insights on these issues.

One Father's Story

One morning I was sitting at the breakfast table with my wife, my three-year-old son, John, and my infant daughter. I watched our baby as she lay in her infant seat and watched the three of us eating. When she looked at my wife, she smiled, for she knew that this was the person who fed her, held her, and made everything all right. She looked at John next and grinned, for her brother was the most wonderful thing in her world. Then she looked at me with a quizzical expression. She wasn't sure what I was doing there. There was another moving thing in her field of view, but what was its purpose?

The past year has been a time of finding a place in my daughter's life. I have been fortunate to be able to spend a lot of time with her, as a father who stays at home with our children. In this time she has discovered that I, too, can be trusted to feed her, change her diapers, and put her to sleep. I am also someone who laughs with her, comforts her when she cries, and plays peekaboo with outstanding skill. In these ways, I have moved from the edge of her life to the center. In her world, she has moved me to a place of importance and even necessity.

The place she has made for me in her world is a lot like

the place I have tried to make for God in my world. God has always been there, but God is not necessarily a part of my life. God can remain on the edge, someone who exists but performs no useful function in my day-to-day life. This is much like the place I originally occupied in the world of my daughter.

Both of us are responsible for my transition from this shadowy presence to a more-full relationship with her. I deliberately stepped into her world, and she gave me a place. In the same way, God has taken a more important role in my life over the past few years. God has continued to take an active part in my life, and I have sought a more active place for God.

I see God showing active concern for me in the larger scope of life and in the day-to-day affairs. I certainly did not intend to become a stay-at-home father when I chose my career. I was in the middle of studies toward a Ph.D. in Old Testament when our first child was born. So I chose to delay completing my education while I took care of John, and now Erin.

Yet this time at home has been invaluable, both for my development as a person and also, I hope, for my future in teaching. Thus God has led me down strange paths, paths I would not have sought out. These paths lead always toward a becoming, to becoming a whole person, a holy person, however far I am from that goal.

Now that I have completed my studies, I find it more difficult to tell people what I do. Earlier I could avoid the issue and say "student," when asked what I do. The question "What do you do?" usually means "What do you do to make money." Being a student is acceptable because it is seen as training toward making money. What I do now as a father has no monetary rewards, and few prospects for advancement. Thus it does not seem to qualify as something worthwhile to *do*.

Part of the difficulty in describing what I do is that the words *father* and *mother* have such different meanings. This is most obvious when we compare fathering (= procreating) with mothering (= caring, protecting). What I am now doing as a father is mothering. I often use the word *parenting* as an alternative. But this suggests that mothering and fathering can be brought together without recognizing the gender differences which our language and culture impose on our expectations.

Often I feel the need to defend my manhood in the face of these expectations. I do that by quickly pointing out my Ph.D., or my interest and participation in sports, or something else that connects me to the *normal* male world.

I have often heard people defend father language for God as being inclusive of the caring and nurturing aspects of God's self. "Fathers are caring, too," they say. Yes, we are, but as a father who has taken on the traditional *mother* role, I know that in our society and in our language, the role of care in the ordinary, mundane tasks of life belongs largely to the mother.

Fathers are expected to be present for the fun times, like learning to throw a ball, to ride a bicycle, or to go camping. They are also expected to be there for the tough times of failure and disappointment. But in the routine tasks of changing diapers and getting lunch ready, the job *belongs* to the mother. Or these are her tasks to delegate to someone else.

This is one place where mother language for God can add to our picture of how God is active in our lives. God is active as a mother in God's constant caring for us in the most routine parts of our lives (Deut. 32:13-14, 18; Ps. 131; Isa. 42:14; 49:1, 5, 14-15; 66:12-13; Luke 15:8-10; Matt. 23:37; John 3:3, 5). You might expect that I, as a stay-at-home father, would defend the use of "Father God" for this role, for I try to live this role out in my life. Yet, as I have just said, we are trapped by our language, which shapes expectations we have of males and females.

One of the ways out of this trap is to begin to use mother language for God. For if the Almighty God is as a mother to us, then surely we cannot devalue the role. Then maybe the role becomes worthwhile, both for women and for men. Certainly part of the problem today is not simply that men feel undervalued for their work as caregivers, but that women feel the same way. So the question is whether *mothering* is a task worthy of God.

The image of God as a mother, then, is useful for me as I become aware of Her presence in my life. In the more ordinary tasks of my day, I see God's hand in providing patience, strength, and especially love. There are so many times when my reserves fail, and I lack the love I need for my children. In these times, God is there, giving strength and guidance.

God's strength and caring are always there, but they become part of the conscious structure of my day as I learn to trust in God's presence. God's actions in my life are not limited by my acknowledgment of them. But my awareness of God's hand enables me to act lovingly when I do not feel particularly loving, to be kind when I would rather be unkind. Thus the awareness of God's presence allows me to tap more easily into the reserves that God supplies.

The awareness of God's presence in my parenting has also changed the way I view God. I used to think of God primarily as one who directs, as one who has a specific will for my life which I must follow, as one who wants something from me. My picture was of a God who was quite task-oriented. Not surprisingly, this picture grew out of the way I approached the world. There were things I wanted to accomplish, and the question was always how to get them done.

As a stay-at-home father, I have become less task-oriented. Children are good at disrupting tasks, getting in the way of schedules, and having accidents or temper tantrums at awkward moments. This is because children live in the present, rather than living in the not-yet of the goals which adults set for themselves. My children have taught me to be more aware of the present, of the needs and concerns of the moment, of the demands of *Right Now*.

As I have been changed, God has also become a greater part of my present. God is the one who cares for me and nurtures me, rather than the one who wants of me or wishes for me. God is not just waiting for me at the goal. Instead, God is a constant companion who wanders with me through the day, even when my day winds along toward no particular goal beside the needs of the moment.

The transformation of my picture of God has been one of which I have been largely unaware. I could not have set it as a goal, since it is a goal which would have stood in the way of the process. The question is not "How do I change my picture of God?" but rather "Where is God in my life right now?" Sometimes the question is more simply "God, where are you?" The trust that comes from God's answer to this question is what nurtures our ongoing relationship, and what sustains me through the task of parenting.

One Mother's Story

In this reflection on being a mother, I talk about how having children changed me. It changed the way I look at myself, my relationship to the world, and my relationship to the God who created us all.

I can remember a particular moment where one change seemed particularly clear. It was at an MCC Women's conference being held at a Catholic retreat center. With me was my daughter, Katie, eight months old. During one of the sessions, she was fussy so I began wandering the halls with her. I came upon the chapel; a huge vaulted space. It was empty except for golden light pouring through giant stained-glass windows.

As I began to walk down the aisle holding my daughter, I thought, "This place is so beautiful. It's the perfect time to truly dedicate my beautiful baby girl to God." But by the time I reached the front, I knew a prayer like that wasn't necessary at all. She was a gift from God, holy and beautiful, and no prayer of dedication was needed. Instead, I prayed, "Thank you for her. Help me always to remember who she is." Holding my baby, I felt more connected to God than I ever had in my entire life.

After each birth, I loved my new baby with a love which engulfed me like a tidal wave. Part of that tidal wave was an awareness of their sacredness, as human beings fresh from God. This knowledge is something which spiraled outward from them. I began to look at myself and the people around me in a new light. I began to see the hand of a creative and loving God in everyone I met.

The freshness and purity of babies may not endure as we grow older, but it's a part of who we are. I came to reverence human life in a different way after I became a parent. I grew to love the verse where Jesus says, "Let the little children come. . . . It is to such as these that the kingdom of heaven belongs" (Matt. 19:14). I felt I had experienced this verse. It did seem to me that God was present in a more transparent way in the early times of my children's lives.

Birthing my two children profoundly changed the way I live in my body. I discovered in a new way the beauty and limitations of who I am as a human body created by God. Pregnancy was a sensory experience which could not be ignored. My sense of smell became acute, food took on a whole new type of meaning as I experienced ravenous hunger pangs, and the rapid changes in the shape and feel of my body amazed me.

I thought about my body image and how I was feeling about the way I looked. I had always thought that a certain shape defined me. While I knew intellectually that I was looking the way a pregnant woman should, I found that I had a hard time loving the way I looked. My faith in God grounded me so that I could say, "This is the way I am, and this is good."

Birthing and nursing reinforced those bodily learnings. My birth experiences made me realize that in spite of all the breathing exercises and resolutions on how I would handle labor, in the end it was an elemental time. My mind retreated, and my body took over. In a similar way, nursing my young changed the way I saw my body. I could produce exactly the nourishment my babies needed at the rate they needed it.

My body's work to birth and feed my children was a holy thing for me and a pleasure hard to describe. I'll never forget the wobbly droopy-eyed look of contentment of my babies after nursing. I could give them what they needed. These bodily things are significant; they have changed the way I view the world. I am a human animal on this earth, created like other animals. I can't forget that. Being a mother has given me an insight into the connectedness of God's creation, and it is changing the way I relate to the world of which I am a part.

I learned other things about my body, things more difficult to accept and more easy to forget, especially now that both my children are older. In a way I hadn't learned before, pregnancy and nursing taught me that the human body has limitations. My body couldn't always do what my mind wanted it to, whether that meant running up a flight of stairs or working nonstop all day. Life became slower. I had to make choices with my body in mind.

While I was nursing my second child, I became ill over and over again until I realized that I wasn't taking care of myself properly. I started consciously setting aside time to rest (hard to arrange, with a crawling baby and an active two-year-old), and then I stopped getting sick. I had to trust God that my home would not fall apart while I rested (and it didn't fall apart; it just got messier!). I learned that it was important to take care of myself and not just the bodies around me.

These understandings of limitations are all lessons which any person with a handicap, or any older person, might think obvious. However, they were new to me as a young, healthy person.

I found the early years of my children to be a lonely

time. This is ironic since the mother-child bond was incredibly intense for me. On one hand, I felt closer to another human being than I ever had in my whole life. Yet on the other hand, the bodily things I was experiencing kept reinforcing how separate we all are. My husband and I love each other. But in the end, it was my body giving birth. He could hold my hand, he couldn't take on my pain.

I could give birth to a baby, but no matter how much I loved her, her life was totally separate from mine. She had a birth experience; I had a giving-birth experience. One day she may hold my hand while I die, but she won't be able to die for me. We have companions, but we're on this journey alone. In this context, the belief in a Friend who knows us completely and never leaves us has been a comfort on which I rely.

I have stayed at home full-time with my children for five years, and I wouldn't trade this for any other experience. It has been delightful, spending so much time with them in their early childhood years. I realize that it's an opportunity that not everyone can take. My enjoyment of these years does not mean that they've been easy. On the contrary, they have been, without a doubt, the most personally challenging years of my life.

I was surprised to find that the tidal wave of love I had for my children has been matched by a tidal wave of demands upon me that I sometimes find hard to handle. I have come to realize I am a person capable of both great love and great anger. Parenting has launched me headfirst into the task of managing myself. The parenting books I read hadn't prepared me for that. I thought parenting was supposed to be about managing children! I have found myself drawing on the subterranean strength inside me which is God's, a strength I haven't always known was there.

I didn't decide to spend five years mothering full-time. It was originally going to be a one- or two-year sabbatical from my doctoral program and a teaching career I was eager to pursue. But each year, staying home was the only choice that felt right for me. Some people are puzzled by my apparent lack of dedication to my career. Yet most friends have been supportive of my decision to stay home with my children. I've found companionship for my work from other mothers, and even from the occasional father, those at home full-time with their children.

Mothering is important and vital work. Yet in spite of my belief in that statement, I have struggled with problems of self-esteem. I can't count how many times I've been asked, "Are you at home, or do you work?" I've never worked so hard in my life, and I am at home! In social settings friends will often go around the table asking how everyone's job is going, but no one thinks to ask how mothering is going. Perhaps people assume they know what mothering is all about. But that is surprising; I often find myself in new and uncharted waters!

I continually struggle with the balance between doing the work which parenting involves, and just being with my children. In the end, these situations help me to reflect on how my sense of self-worth needs to be wrapped up in my faith. I believe in a God who, like a mother, accepts me and loves me for who I am, not for what I do.

All of the mothering experiences I've described here are directly related to my relationship with God. They are the context out of which I pray, they are the questions I bring to God. Being a parent has become part of my psalm of praise.

What Do You Think?

1. What words come to mind when you think of the word fathering? the word mothering? If you are a parent, how does this affect how you see yourself as a father or a mother? Are you more comfortable imaging God as a father or a mother?

2. How are stay-at-home parents encouraged by your church community? Is the church as supportive of men taking full-time long-term care of their children as they are of women doing this?

3. When parents of young children work outside the home, are they affirmed and supported by your church community?

4. For those of you who have given birth, how or what did that experience teach you about God?

5. How can loving children change the lives of people who don't have children of their own?

If You Want to Read More

Gerson, Kathleen. *Hard Choices: Women Decide About Work, Career, and Motherhood.* Univ. of Calif. Press, 1986.

Hebblethwaite, Margaret. *Motherhood and God.* Geoffrey Chapman UK, Morehouse Pub., 1994.

Rich, Adrienne. *Of Women Born: Motherhood as Experience and Institution.* W. W. Norton, 1976.

Ruddick, Sara. *Maternal Thinking: Toward a Politics of Peace.* Beacon Press, 1989.

Van Leeuwen, Mary Stewart. *Love, Work and Parenting in a Changing World.* InterVarsity, 1990.

11

Raising Nonsexist Children

Atlee Beechy

Atlee Beechy is a retired psychology and peace studies professor at Goshen (Ind.) College. He is married to Winifred Nelson, and they have three daughters, four granddaughters, and two grandsons. He has been active in MCC relief and peace ministries and continues his witness through Seniors for Peace.

RAISING CHILDREN is a challenge. Raising nonsexist children in today's materialistic, violent, and still largely patriarchal world is daunting. Anyone who thinks they know enough to advise others on how to do it must be out of touch with reality, have a streak of arrogance, have never raised children or finished raising them, or have enough interest in and concern for the future to risk the vulnerability involved.

This also is an emotional topic. We differ in our understandings of the Scriptures. Our experiences have influenced our positions. Let us be respectful and patient with each other as we try to find our way. I tread uneasily into this territory.

Because I recognize my limitations, I turned to sixteen wise and cooperative friends for help: middle school, high school, and college students; parents experienced in raising nonsexist children, a Christian education director, a pastor, a New Testament scholar, two early childhood specialists, a medical doctor, two mental health specialists, and student development and campus ministry staff. Their good counsel and many of their suggestions have been incorporated in this paper.

I learned much through the years from my wife, three daughters, and four granddaughters as to what it means to be female in today's sexually twisted and discriminating society. Since I grew up with two brothers and no sisters, I needed some corrective education! I also drew from faith centered in God's reconciling work and call, my graduate studies in psychology, my students, and my counseling experiences.

My overall objective is to help us become more aware of the nature of sexist prejudice and discrimination, their early beginnings, and their impact on children. This involves examining how Jesus and other biblical writers viewed children and the kingdom, and discussing factors that create sexist prejudice and discrimination. I conclude with ten suggestions for your consideration in working at this pervasive problem.

Jesus valued and welcomed children. In Matthew 19:13-15, Jesus countermands his disciples' efforts to keep the children away: "Let the little children come to me, and do not stop them; for it is to such as these that the kingdom of heaven belongs." Jesus lifts up their openness, innocence, trust, and forgiveness patterns as models for all who follow him.

In Mark 9:36-37, Jesus takes a child into his arms and teaches his disciples about humility, true greatness, and hospitality: "Whoever welcomes one such child in my name welcomes me, and whoever welcomes me welcomes not me but the one who sent me." In Mark 9:42, Jesus warns those who offend the little ones in strong words: "If any of you put a stumbling block before one of these little ones who believe in me, it would be better for you if a great millstone were hung around your neck and you were thrown into the sea."

According to Matthew 5 and other Scriptures, Jesus lived and taught the biblical themes of grace, discipleship, compassion, justice, forgiveness, reconciliation, humility, community, and respect for all of the human family, even those called enemies. For me, these are wonderful gifts to show God's way for us in all relationships and situations.

Our Problem

Are sexism, racism, and all forms of prejudice and discrimination "stumbling blocks" that often are placed in overburdened hearts of children today? Seeds of prejudice and discrimination are sown early. A perceptive international student says, "They are put into their hearts when they are young and helpless." A few examples will help define the problem.

• Who hasn't heard or used the following words? "He is all boy. Don't be a sissy! Little boys don't cry or play with dolls. Little girls don't play with cars and trucks."

• A fifteen-year-old boy wants to become a nurse, takes the taunts of his peers, and finds no support at school or at home.

• An eleven-year-old girl is troubled when her teacher strongly discourages her from exploring a nontraditional vocational interest.

• A five-year-old girl's mother tells her, "When you say grace, you could say, 'Let us thank Her for our food,' because God isn't a man or a woman. You can say He or She." The little girl laughs and says, "Oh, Mom, that's silly. Everyone knows God is a man."

• A mother was critical of her ten-year-old son who had the habit of not picking up after himself. In firm tones she said, "What are you going to do when you don't have me to pick up after you?" After a moment, the son said, "I am going to marry someone who will do my picking up." Later he added, "I guess I really don't want to marry someone who is that stupid."

• A college male responded to a letter on the student opinion board calling for more mutual respect and equality in female-male relationships. He scribbled on its margin, "What's the problem? Women were created to serve men."

These are all seeds that do not bear good fruit.

Webster defines sexism as "attitudes and behaviors based on traditional stereotypes of sexual roles; discrimination or devaluation based on a second meaning of a person's sex." In our context, to be sexist means to have prejudicial attitudes and to express discriminatory behaviors—treating the other sex condescendingly, unfairly, or violently. Such expressions restrict the healthy growth of all involved: those discriminated against, and those doing the discriminating.

Those with sexist attitudes are imprisoned in their own cells of insecurity, self-righteousness, ignorance, twisted thinking, and distorted faith. The contemporary snapshots listed above clearly reflect sexist language and behaviors—sex domination, superior attitudes, manipulation, power misuse, ego arrogance, distortions of masculinity and femininity, and disrespect for personhood.

Nonsexist certainly does not mean a neutral sexuality, denying our gender, or demanding uniformity in behavior. Instead, nonsexist means understanding, accepting, and rejoicing in our gender and sexuality, and viewing and valuing both sexes equally. It means helping members of both sexes to create and participate in relationships and in institutions marked by mutual respect, compassion, and justice for all.

This includes acceptance, respect, and support for single people, often left out, with their needs ignored. Women and men who choose full-time parenting or select some cooperative pattern also deserve our respect and support.

Factors That Generate Sexist Attitudes and Behavior

"Don't let the world around you squeeze you into its own mold, but let God remold your minds from within" (Rom. 12:2, Phillips). "What does the Lord require of you but to do justice, and to love kindness, and to walk humbly with your God?" (Mic. 6:8).

We face three issues in dealing with this topic: nature versus nurture, differences between girls and boys, and how these relate to their role socialization. Nature versus nurture was an issue in the time of Confucius (500 B.C.) and remains a lively topic in social science gatherings today. Lawrence Wright reviewed many studies of twins and asks, "Are we the victims of our genes or of our environment?" He refers to "ingrained or inborn tendencies" and concludes, "It makes little difference how such tendencies were acquired, only how they are managed" (see list below).

I believe both nature and nurture are important in human development. I do not believe, however, that we can blame genetics for our prejudices and our discriminatory behavior, or credit inheritance for our nonsexist attitudes and behavior. Nurture builds on the potentials that genetic factors provide and is of primary concern in this article.

In Western societies, boys are characterized as strong, aggressive, independent, competitive, less emotional, and more logical and direct than girls. Girls are characterized as passive, emotional, loving, sensitive, and nurturing. They are also seen as more verbal, dependent, and social than boys. Roles are then prescribed on the basis of these assumed different characteristics of boys and girls. Children are socialized to accept these roles and shuttled toward them: girls to be good teachers and nurturers, and boys to be administrators and engineers.

Maccoby and Jacklin list five physiological gender differences: body build, muscular development, hormonal patterns, child-bearing capacity, and longevity. Some research indicates that boys are more aggressive in their behavior, and that girls mature more rapidly in the earlier years. These findings show some differences between girls and boys in school subject performances but not in basic intelligence.

There are a number of unclear areas. Evidence indicates that the range of traits, including emotional, is greater within each sex than on average between the two genders. There is increasing interest in having desirable human traits in common, across the gender border. Love, empathy, sensitivity, and kindness are desirable human traits and should not be viewed only as feminine. Similarly, logical thinking, decisiveness, frankness, and organizational ability should not be viewed only as male traits but as desirable human traits.

Our God is beyond gender. In our limitations, we can only describe God with the strongest and most praiseworthy human characteristics that we can imagine. If the movement toward nonsexism can happen more fully, everyone will benefit. There will be greater use of ability potentials. Deeper and richer emotional experiences become available. Greater fairness and mutuality will be achieved, leading to lowered tensions, hostility, and fear levels as well as better morale.

Some of the factors that impact sexist attitudes and behaviors:

• Societal values and patterns: materialism, militarism, violence, depersonalization, and fragmentation.

• Patriarchy, defined by Webster as "a social organization marked by supremacy of the father in the clan or family, the legal dependence of wives and children, and the reckoning of descent and inheritance in the male line." This concept certainly continues to keep sexist attitudes and discrimination alive in family and institutional structures.

• Family climate, parent modeling and teachings, and parent relationships to each other and their children. The early years are particularly important.

• School climate and experiences: peer and teacher

modeling and teachings, prejudiced and unbalanced curriculum materials, too much emphasis on competitiveness, single-gender games, and toys and games that encourage violence and sexist behavior.

• Media: TV, radio, books, magazines, videos, cartoons, advertisements. We are just beginning to understand the tremendous power these greed-driven factors have in shaping our children's sexual attitudes and behaviors.

• Lack of congregational awareness of the nature and pervasiveness of our problem, as well as lack of commitment and shortage of constructive biblical plans to work toward nonsexist relationship patterns in congregational life. This means serious study and revision of certain areas: biblical language and interpretation, Sunday school curriculum and library resources on sexist attitudes and behaviors, the pattern and content of worship, and gender makeup and modeling of congregational leadership staff.

• Sexist language used in home, school, and congregation.

• Preferential treatment of one gender by parents, teachers, counselors, or administrators. Some research has shown that such behavior by adult caregivers may lead boys to aggressively taunt and tease girls, and girls to unduly use charm to manipulate boys. Neither fully respects the personality and personhood of the other gender. Thus girls may feel inferior, resulting in lower self-confidence. Boys may slip into an artificial superiority mentality, underlaid by insecurity.

Ten Suggestions for Working at Reducing Sexism
The factors listed above are somewhat frightening. The world is trying "to squeeze you into its own mold." Some of these factors have potential for helping to reduce sexist attitudes and behaviors, but most are controlled by those who hold power and believe in materialistic gods. This conflict has the appearance of a David-Goliath encounter!

The Chinese have a saying, "Unless you change directions, you will end up where you are headed." It is time to change our directions. The following list of things to do is not inclusive. You may add or subtract goals. Decide your priorities, and get involved! Keep hope and humor alive!

1. I begin by first facing my own sexist attitudes and behaviors. I have discovered and continue to discover sexism in my attitudes and behaviors. I am becoming aware of how deeply patriarchy is embedded and how it impacts my inner self and my responses. I feel a continuing need for a deepened experience in God's comforting and confronting grace. This continuing conversion process never ends. I also need the support of sisters and brothers to keep me accountable in my efforts to free myself from sexist attitudes and behaviors.

2. Follow Jesus' example in highly valuing and affirming children. Let our affirmations come liberally, along with loving discipline.

3. Give high priority to parenting, nurturing, and meeting the basic needs of our children, so they can:

• Be loved and love.

• Understand and respect themselves and understand and respect those of the other gender.

• Know and feel God's love coming from those around them, and learn to share that love.

• Be treated fairly, and treat others fairly.

• Discover how girls and boys are the same and how they differ, and know that both are important, equally valued in God's family.

• Know and socialize and have fun with members of their own sex and with the other gender.

• Develop a healthy sense of personal and group identity.

Meeting these basic needs strengthens the inner sense of self-worth and confidence so necessary for resisting the world's efforts to force us into its mold!

4. Participate in planning and carrying out congrega-

tional preventive and corrective educational programs that work at the problems outlined in factor 6 in the list of what generates sexist attitudes and behaviors.

5. Develop a positive gender-valuing and gender-affirming climate in our homes. This can be done in many ways: parents modeling the expression of love, respect, and fairness; sharing parenting and daily maintenance responsibilities; providing regular family council opportunities where children can share their joys, hurts, questions, and counsel comfortably. Provide help for children who have suffered the pain of discrimination to move beyond victimization and survival. Show them how they can constructively aid in the battle against sexist attitudes and behaviors. Use family worship, prayers at any time, and bedtime stories that awaken dreams and build up inner strength and convictions. Provide settings where both girls and boys have opportunity to achieve and to lead.

6. Participate in efforts to help our schools develop a positive gender climate. This can be done by avoiding instructional groupings based on gender and destructive competitiveness; providing greater emphasis on cooperative learning and multicultural education; incorporating gender balance and richness in library holdings and all teaching-learning materials; and selecting teaching staff and administrative personnel who in fairness offer equal respect, love, opportunity, and value to all girls and all boys.

7. Provide settings where persons who violate children through sexist attitudes and behaviors can be confronted, and where helpful follow-up discussions, actions, and resources are provided.

8. Begin or join a group which monitors TV and other media programming for sexist images and stories, and puts pressure on violating companies to change their ways. Affirm companies and programs demonstrating responsibility in this field.

9. Use role reversals as teaching tools, and provide games, songs, and activities that cross sex lines and teach

respect for both genders.

10. Start the education early. Discuss gender issues before marriage. Remember that infants pick up feelings and attitudes very early and sense whether they are valued or not valued, and what behaviors are expected of them.

Summary

I believe that sexist attitudes and behaviors are sins and are contrary to Jesus' teachings on relationships and the new community. They are divisive and destructive to the individual, the family, the congregation, the school, the workplace, and society. They often generate apathy, anger, alienation, depression, or violence. They also stifle curiosity and inhibit learning.

Congregations need to do much more in providing support and resources for those who have been hurt by sexist attitudes and behaviors. Those who violate children physically or psychologically often have deeply rooted needs and problems. They usually need confrontation and spiritual and professional help.

Under certain circumstances, victims may wish to be involved in confrontations. This has potential for being a growth experience for them if they can confront in a creative, direct, nonviolent way. Some children are learning this approach in school. Confrontational encounters can also be revealing and helpful to violators, who often need a deepened experience in God's grace to get on the road to change.

As an alternative to patriarchy, Riane Eisler recommends a model "in which social relations are primarily based on the principle of linking rather than ranking, and may best be described as the partnership model. In this model—beginning with the most fundamental difference . . . between male and female—diversity is not equated with either inferiority or superiority" (xvii). Jesus also calls us to an alternative way of relating. Jesus, the Servant, is our model for life in the transformed community.

The pace forward is slow, but there is movement toward a less-sexist new community marked by respect, acceptance, mutuality in service, justice, trust, and love for everyone. Let us not retreat to apathy, cynicism, hate, or despair. Let us keep hope alive and move forward with God's help and the support of each other! Emily Greene Balch, winner of 1946 Nobel Peace Prize, has good words for us: "We have a long, long way to go. So let us hasten along the road, the roads of human tenderness and generosity. Groping, we may find one another's hand in the dark."

Prayer

God, we thank you for your amazing, healing, and empowering grace. Let your grace penetrate our minds and hearts. Free us from fear, guilt, hate, and the need to dominate and control. Fill us with gentleness, courage, hope, trust, joy, patience, compassion, and respect for what you are doing in us and in others. Guide us as we join our children in finding your way of relating that moves from domination to genuine partnership in our homes, schools, and congregations. Amen.

What Do You Think?

1. How does Jesus view children and relationships within the family?

2. Are girls and boys equally accepted, respected, and valued in our families? In our congregations, schools, and society? Why? Why not?

3. How do children learn about themselves, their gender, their similarities and differences, and their roles? How do they learn to respect those who are different?

4. What factors generate prejudicial attitudes and discriminatory behaviors?

5. How can we help children unlearn destructive attitudes toward themselves and the other gender, to develop freeing, constructive Christlike gender attitudes and behaviors?

If You Want to Read More

Aldredge, Joan. *A Word for Girls and Boys.* Glad River Publications, 1993.

Balch, Emily Greene. In *Seeds of Peace: A Catalogue of Quotations*, 113. Ed. Jeanne Larson and Madge Cyrus-Micheels. New Society Publishers, 1986.

Cecil, Nancy Lee. *Raising Peaceful Children in a Violent World.* LuraMedia, 1995.

Eisler, Riane. *The Chalice and the Blade.* Harper & Row, 1982.

_____ and Loye, David. *The Partnership Way.* Harper & Row, 1990.

Maccoby, Eleanor Emmons, and Carol Nagy Jacklin. *The Psychology of Sex Differences.* Stanford Univ. Press, 1974. Findings summarized in *Psychology Today,* Dec. 1974.

McGinnis, James and Kathleen. *Parenting for Peace and Justice: Ten Years Later.* Rev. ed. Orbis Books, 1990.

Tannen, Deborah. *You Just Don't Understand: Women and Men in Conversation.* Ballantine Books, 1990.

Turner, Glennette Tilley. *Take a Walk in Their Shoes.* Dutton, Cobblehill Books, 1989.

Wehrheim, Carol A. *The Great Parade: Learning About Women, Justice and the Church*, with teacher's guide and children's activity pages. Friendship Press, 1992.

Wright, Lawrence. *New Yorker,* Oct. 3, 1995.

12

Youth and Gender Relationships

Joan Yoder

*Joan Yoder lives in Rosthern, Saskatchewan. She gradu-
ated from Goshen (Ind.) College with a social work
degree and worked as dean of students at Rosthern Junior
College for twelve years. She is married to Eric Yoder,
and they have two adult sons. She has been active in education on family violence issues, and is helping to manage a tea room and arts center in her community.*

Amy's Dream

TREVOR AND I were best friends. Trevor told me that if I
pushed myself high enough on my swing set, I could touch
God with my toes. I believed him. I told Trevor that dirt tast-
ed like chocolate. He believed me (until he tried it).

When we were seven, we decided that neither of us
would ever marry. Instead, we would live in a mansion in
California, where it was always warm. We would eat chocolate bars for breakfast, lunch, and supper.

One crisp September evening, Trevor came to me and

said, "Amy, we can't be friends anymore. Darren says that now that we're in grade six, everyone thinks I'm a wimp for having a girl for my best friend. The only time that I'm supposed to talk to a girl is if she's my girlfriend." He shrugged his shoulders as if it was no big deal.

"What does Darren know, anyhow?" I asked vehemently. "Besides, why can't you just pretend I'm your girlfriend. Secretly, we'll just be friends of course," I added with emphasis. "Sorry, Amy, but it doesn't work that way. Everyone knows that boyfriends and girlfriends have to kiss," said my ex-best friend. He then turned and walked away. I moved to the other side of town that December, and I never saw Trevor again.

After that day, my outlook was drastically changed. Never have I stopped wondering why the level of equality and respect is so severely lowered between boys and girls as they grow older. As I see it, the relationship is lost through a chain reaction. Fear of being different causes miscommunication, which causes misunderstanding, which eventually causes lack of respect. They say that maturity comes with age. Why then do we tend to find it easier to treat each other with respect when we are kids?

I deeply pondered this question the summer before my grade-twelve year. There I sat on a swing in my neighborhood playground. The sun's rays warmed me, and my ears were filled with the sounds of children at play. Something came over me, and I began to swing. Back and forth, I pumped my legs with fervor. The wind felt cool and exhilarating on my face. I stretched my toes high into the sky, hoping to touch God.

—*Amy, in grade twelve*

Childhood is a time of magic. Experiences from that time of our life set the stages on which we play out our lives. The magic spell of childhood creates both heaven and hell. Consequently, we are both drawn toward and repelled by similar plays in later life.

In our Western society, teenagers have a slice of time,

and they must try to make sense of it before the demands and responsibilities of adulthood set in. Bombarded from the wings with myriads of props, teens construct specific sets on which to play out various roles. In these scenarios, we observe a sense of simplicity and integrity, crafted by the soul of the teenager.

Often we judge the messages we hear to be somewhat naive. As adults, we know that experience casts a certain gray ambiance over the clear understandings and definitions of youth. As we take time to listen to teenagers, let us remember our own teen years. Then let us learn of their current world, acknowledging that they hold in their hands visions which light the way of hope for today, and the future.

I am fascinated by young women such as Amy, raised by feminist mothers who believe that men and women have equal rights, potentials, and responsibilities in the living out of daily life. As I listen to Amy recount a favorite childhood memory, and then recall its demise, I am saddened. I know this may well be the beginning of Amy playing out a coquettish role. That role is foisted on her by a society in which males are required to "make the rules" that dictate how they and females relate.

Amy's mother has made a life for herself and her daughter, because she could no longer remain healthy living life according to another's dictates. I listen to Amy reflect on how her own male friends think she's too assertive and opinionated, and therefore "not compatible." I admire Amy's strong sense of self.

I wonder if Amy will find strong, healthy role models in the area of gender relations. I hope such model persons will be able to teach communication skills that allow for vigorous give-and-take, and openness to another's thinking. Then she can learn patience, love, toleration, humor, gentleness, willingness to admit one's errors, and the ability to stand firm in one's own strengths.

Bart's Dilemmas

Listen to Bart's story. Bart finds himself in a home with three sisters and his mom. His father died when he was twelve. Bart often feels lonely. It seems to him that everyone is vying for each other's attention. He often feels hurt as the battle for attention wages. But he does feel good about one thing. He is a good listener; consequently, his sisters and mother confide in him, sharing their vulnerabilities, hurts, and fears with him.

This casts him in the role of caregiver and potential protector. However, it all becomes too much for him when his sisters' boyfriends start using them in selfish, abusive manners. Bart takes to drinking, and acting out in an aggressive macho manner toward the boyfriends.

This demeanor carries over into his high school life, where it is not tolerated. Positive productivity in school becomes an issue, and his mother is advised to consider sending him to a private church school. There he may be able again to let his better side come out, away from the pressures of the home setting.

Now in a residential high school setting, some girls risk being honest with Bart. He quickly learns that they are not impressed with his *tough-guy* act. He thinks this over and continues to talk with the girls, enjoying the honest give-and-take in the conversations. He begins to feel that he too can share with them how various events impact on him.

As Bart starts sharing his feelings of hurt, loneliness, fear, and anger, he begins to realize that he really is quite a loving, gentle person. However, he still gets upset about guys who talk of their girlfriends in a crude, exploitative manner. He knows that he should voice his revulsion of such talk. But he fears becoming the laughingstock of the *cool dudes*. So he remains quiet. There is only one other guy with whom he feels safe to share his real feelings and opinions.

I have a soft spot in my heart for young men of Bart's kind. Some young cool-dude macho *actors* do become vulnerable persons who acknowledge their own sensitivities with people who care enough not to give up on them. When I see that happen, I gain hope that change is possible. I am encouraged by young men and women who dare to take a stand with each other, challenging each other in areas where they sense a lack of wholeness or honesty.

Can we as adults also be open to such encounters? I fear that too often we act falsely for the sake of economic or political expediency. In gender relations, this can frequently mean denying our individual strengths and sensitivities. What kind of role modeling are we providing for the teenagers among us?

Amy and Bart are children from single-parent homes. As they process what it means to be in relationship with the opposite sex, they both treasure those times in their lives when their own whole selves have been honored. They long for further opportunities through which they can realize (make real) that person within themselves whom they themselves know and love.

Amy and Bart have in their teen years both known and honored to some extent those values which they know to be life-giving for themselves and others. Will experiences in the future provide them with gender roles that honor whole persons? Or will they be coerced by the demands of life's stages into playing false roles which alienate them from the image of the Creator within them?

While working with teenagers, I become confounded by the number of girls who devour Harlequin romances and live for the next episode of their favorite soap opera. They tell me that their mothers do the same. I find it hard not to be too judgmental of girls who go to bizarre lengths to capture the attention of certain young men.

They feel they are nothing if they do not have a boyfriend, and they engage in facade-making activities. They lose touch with those qualities and interests which are uniquely theirs. It makes me wonder how and where they have learned such values. Too often I have seen that such false images of love lead to future marital breakdown.

Vivian's Quest

I feel bombarded on every side . . .
  . . . Gender issues
. . . Homosexuality
 . . . Violence against women
 . . . Feminism.

What does all of it mean?
I don't understand.
How does it affect me now?
I am so confused.
How will it affect me in twenty years?

All I ask is that I might be able
 to love and be loved,
 to speak and be heard,
 to accept and be accepted.

—*Vivian, a senior in high school*

Vivian has a group of close girlfriends with whom she processes the issues that arise in her life. Because of the support, sharing, and affirmation which she receives from this group, Vivian is able to live creatively, productively, and happily. However, she is aware that some of her male peers speculate that she may be gay, because she hangs around with a group of girls and doesn't go out with guys. This information is unsettling for Vivian.

She is not aware that through the ages, women have been denied the opportunity of getting together with other women, sometimes in subtle, sometimes in not-so-subtle ways. When groups of women operate in life-giving ways with confidence, they at times threaten men who hold positions of authority, power, and economic privilege.

Vivian's scenario provides us with an insight into the subtle ways our society holds supposedly life-giving gender roles in place. Our children and teenagers learn to play the roles and speak the scripts without understanding what power structures they are maintaining and authorizing. Sadly, only later in life, when they are suffocating because they have been so cut off from the life-giving force within themselves, do they begin to struggle to find out what is going on.

I would like to see the educators in our schools and churches become intimately informed about death-dealing power structures, pass on the knowledge, and then together with young and old alike, envision life-giving scripts.

What role will female friends have for Vivian in the future? How do the boys' comments make Vivian feel about her sexuality? What roles will females and males play in Vivian's life in years to come?

I know that young people such as Vivian are highly conscious that there are many things not right with the world. Vivian has seen injustices while overseas with her parents on an MCC assignment. She has seen inequities here at home in North America. She is an alert and aware young person, actively opening herself to new understandings and experiences.

I respect her longing for mutual loving, healthy communication and acceptance. I hope that she finds adults who have enough energy to engage in this journey with her. We want to keep on discovering new truths regarding unjust death-dealing systems. To do this, we must not bury our heads in the sands of affluence and the comforts it provides.

I fear that a faulty theology may lead us to think that somehow we deserve this good life because we are living right. This utopian *right* is reflected in Vivian's last verse. It is sad if we only pursue such rights and close our eyes to whether or not these rights have anything to do with the issues named in Vivian's first verse.

Rob's Solution
Giving Voice

> Healthy human relationships can be the most difficult goal
> that any of us ever strive for in life. In school they teach you
> physics, literature, history, performance art, auto mechanics,
> and a score of other important things. When it comes to
> building relationships, however, you're on your own. There
> are no classes you can take, no assignments you can do.
> Hope lies in the adage that experience is the best teacher.
> —*Rob, two years after high school*

This section of the book speaks about relationships
between the sexes, either in the form of love or of friendship.
I'm going to broaden the scope because I think the same standard applies to all human interaction. We need to ponder relationships across gender, across race, across faith, across generation, across sexuality, across different understandings in the
world—and then consider our place in the world.
Communication is what joins all of these.

All relationships are opportunities to learn and to grow,
but none more so than when we strive for love and base our
friendships on love. Teach each other to communicate. Allow
each other to learn. Admit your failings, and celebrate your
successes. Deal with problems in your relationships fully and
openly. Listen. Do not seek to convince but to understand. Be
honest. Remember that no one can read your mind.

Above all, take time to listen to each other's voice. Learn
that skill, and apply it to all aspects of your life. Give God a
voice. Give voice to those that love you. Give voice to those that
hate you, who don't understand you, who persecute you. Give
voice to yourself, to who you are. And in the midst of all those
voices, take the wonderful opportunity to sit back and listen.

Teenagers, gender relationships, dating—the scene is
full of interconnections for all involved. As adults, let us hear

the hopes of teenagers. Let us rejoice in their idealism. Let us dare to act on their suggestions. As we listen to the individual stories that arise from their experiences, let us not forget that we were their first models.

Let us as adults educate ourselves by reading books that help us think about youth and gender relationships. Let us read the Bible again and retell the stories of the women, and strive to understand the roles they played. Then let us tell the whole story in our Sunday school classes, believing that the whole picture will create potential for holy living.

Let us not get so caught up in the surface goings on of teenage relationships that we forget that the outward manifestations of teenage angst (distress) and joy are a call to listen to the story that teenagers are hearing. Amy, Bart, Vivian, and Rob are honoring their truths. In their lives, they and many of their peers have resonated with the Giver and Creator of Life in their lives.

Gender roles and relationships are undergoing paradigm shifts. This is not an easy time for teenagers as they try to explore new models of life-giving mutuality. Perhaps the best we can do is to say amen to them when they share with us their life-giving experiences. Those events have given them a sense of peace, happiness, and courage to pursue wholeness for themselves and others.

What Do You Think?

1. After reading about Amy, Bart, Vivian and Rob, identify and name your initial reactions to what they have to say.

2. Name the life-giving qualities these young people value.

3. Knowing what each of these young people honors, role-play with someone in your group a dialogue which you could have with one of these youth. Assume that you have just heard of some event in the teen's life which seems to oppose the values the youth holds.

4. What could you share from your life experience with these young people that would illustrate and affirm their values? Use illustrations which involve gender relationships. Don't be afraid to talk about times in your life when a "lack" of these values surfaced. Work at being open to advice that young people might offer to you.

If You Want to Read More

Miedziar, Myrian. *Boys Will Be Boys*. Doubleday, Anchor Books, 1991.

Pipher, Mary. *Reviving Ophelia: Saving the Selves of Adolescent Girls*. Ballantine Books, 1994.

13

Gender in the Church

Frances Hiebert

Frances Hiebert lives in Mundelein, Illinois. She and her husband, Paul, attend North Suburban Mennonite Church. She is director of student services at Trinity Evangelical Divinity School in Deerfield, Illinois. Frances and Paul have three adult children and four grandchildren.

I WAS BORN in 1934, so I have lived through a time when there has been much conflict and struggle over the role of women in church and society. I know firsthand the pain and frustration of being carefully taught the Christian faith and then being denied entrance to certain kinds of study and ministry. That happened because I was born female and became a woman.

From the time I was a small child, I had a passion for theology and often approached a pastor with some question about his sermon—and it was his in those days, not her.

Before I was a teenager, this was considered cute. But when I was older, I sensed that in my church, that interest was considered inappropriate for a girl.

When I was growing up, *male* and *masculine* still were deeply imbedded in our culture as the norm for what was human. Even when the winds of change began to blow, there was no discussion of *the role of men* because they were the standard for *normal* human beings. The question was whether women could live up to that standard. Many changes have occurred for women since that time, but we still are struggling for the full affirmation of our personhood, especially in the area of leadership in the church.

Due to the traditional attitude toward women in many churches, some women have decided that God is against them. Others blame the church for misunderstanding God and Scripture. The issue of the role of women has caused many women to question who they are in relation to God and the church.

A widely quoted little girl's prayer poignantly points to the ambivalence and discrimination often experienced by women. The little girl prayed, "Dear God, are boys better than girls? I know you are one [a boy], but try to be fair. Sylvia" (Aldredge, 10; see list below). How have we gotten to this place where a child would see female as something that God is not?

The Sins of the Fathers
We can find some of the roots of discrimination against women in the writings of the Greek and Roman *church fathers* from the second century onward. These were converts to Christian faith who had been indoctrinated in classical Greek philosophy. They brought Greek assumptions about the inferiority of women into the church and used them to interpret Christian doctrines.

The early church fathers were concerned to present

Christianity in a way that was acceptable to the surrounding cultures. They wanted to stop persecution of Christians and to make converts. By the middle of the fourth century, they had become quite successful. Emperor Constantine had come out publicly in favor of Christianity. The church became fashionable. This dealt a mortal blow to Paul's great Christian manifesto of human equality in Galatians 3:28.

Paul Bristow writes,

> As the church became more and more transformed by the world, its life took on more of the characteristics of Hellenized Roman society. Slowly the teachings of Greek philosophy interbred with Christian theology, producing a brood of beliefs that were often pagan in their assumptions. (72-73)

In the same vein, the French writer Jacques Ellul writes that the church's acquisition of wealth and success caused it to set aside Christian values of grace, love, and nonviolence. He believes that these are the innovative elements in Christianity and are more strongly represented by women. Instead, the church adopted values of power, glory, conquest, and domination. As a result, women's position was lowered in the church. This was justified by the use of biblical texts taken out of context and removed from the larger theological picture.

The writings of the Patristic period about women seem shocking today, even to those who hold a "traditional" position. For example, Tertullian wrote, "Woman, . . . you are the devil's gateway. . . . You destroyed so easily God's image in man. On account of your desert [deserved punishment]—death—even the Son of God had to die" (Bristow, 116).

The thirteenth-century theologian Thomas Aquinas was a brilliant theologian. But on the nature of women, he agreed with Aristotle: Woman "is defective and misbegotten." Largely because of how Aquinas interpretated Paul's writings through Aristotle's eyes, the doctrine of women's inferiority has persisted in Christian theology (Ellul, 28-29, 115).

From our perspective today, there is a sinister aspect to the demeaning of women. That is the driving force behind what has been described above. Some brave Christian writers and speakers are pointing to Satan as the one who constantly tries to defeat God's plan of equality and mutual support between men and women.

Paul Smith, a Southern Baptist pastor, writes that there is definitely a war going on against women. But it is not a war of men against women. The cause of the war is Satan, who is fighting against both sexes and uses the fallen powers and principalities of this world to keep us in oppressive traditions and structures (106-107). Sadly, the church often has not been able to discern the enemy, who is disguised as an *angel of light* and has used religious arguments to justify the war on women.

The Effect of Language: Is God's Robe Pink or Blue?

Little Sylvia believed that God is "a boy" and therefore likes boys better than girls. That distortion is strongly reinforced by the authoritative, constantly repeated religious language of the church. It is also perpetuated in the hidden assumptions of the English language that the male is the standard for real humanity.

Language both reflects and influences attitudes toward women and men. In many ways, standard English reflects the attitudes of the white middle-class male. It mirrors the sexism in our society. This can be proved by the many negative terms for women, words rarely or never used for men (such as *prostitute*), the use of first names more often for women, and the use of titles more often for men (Frank and Anshen, 5-6).

In a recent lecture series at our school, the speaker and his wife were introduced a number of times as Dr. Smith and his wife, Jane (names changed). Never once did anyone refer to her as Dr. Jane Smith, although she has two earned doctoral degrees.

Language, however, is not only a mirror. According to some linguists, the grammatical structure may actually influence the thought of those who speak that language (Frank and Anshen, 63). When grown women are called girls, it reinforces their dependent, secondary status. When I was 54 years old, I walked into a shoe store, holding my 24-month-old granddaughter by the hand. The clerk, who looked to be about 17 years old, asked cheerfully, "What can I do for you girls today?"

In spite of the movement toward inclusive language throughout our society, why is it still impossible to devise gender-neutral pronouns? Is it because we still accept what the deep structure of our language teaches us—that male is what is really and fully human?

The issue of inclusive language in the church today has two major parts. One is inclusive language for people; the other is inclusive language for God. Some progress has been made on inclusive language for people, probably because it is not as threatening as such language for God.

Still, occasionally Scripture is read from an older translation that retains the inherent bias of the English language toward the masculine gender. This translation has often restricted or obscured the inclusiveness of the original text (Metzger, xi).

Several times I have heard a Scripture passage expounded beautifully. Then I felt like I was kicked in the stomach when it was applied only in male terminology. I was exhilarated by the beauty of the passage, only to feel that the speaker didn't mean me. In the seminary where I work, we still hear speakers addressing our students of both sexes as "you men."

Excuses given for not using inclusive language for people include that it "sounds awkward," "I love the old hymns just as they are," or "it may be divisive." But do these excuses justify ignoring the personhood of half the human race?

Then there is the question of language for God.

Christian theology, almost without exception, teaches that God is neither male nor female. God is Spirit and beyond human gender. In Hosea 11:9, God clearly says, "I am God and no mortal." Yet Sylvia and many, many others believe that God is male.

It is true that God is neither male nor female. Yet Genesis 1:27 clearly states that both men and women are made in the image of God. Our human cultures, however, have divided human characteristics into those they think are *feminine* and others they think are *masculine*. By choosing all the *masculine* traits as more characteristic of God, they have made God into a male and denied or played down the *feminine* characteristics of God.

Shouldn't the church be true to its theology of the nature of God rather than accepting a distorted "traditional" concept of God that comes from patriarchal human culture? Paul Smith declares, "Until there is peace between male and female in our image of God, there will be no peace between male and female in the church" (151).

How can we correct this unbalanced concept of the nature and image of God without causing strong adverse reaction in the church? Surely it is a process of education, and probably it must be done in small steps.

I believe the first important step is to recognize that the Bible itself refers to God not only in masculine terms. The passages that portray God as a woman are there as well and need to be studied. In a number of places in the Bible, God or God's Spirit is described as "giving birth" or expressing motherly caring (Deut. 32:18; Isa. 42:14; 49:1, 5, 14-15; John 1:13; 3: 3, 5; 1 Pet. 1:3). The New Testament images God as a woman who searches for a lost coin (Luke 15:8-10). Jesus describes himself as like a mother hen (Matt. 23:37).

Smith lists other steps to be taken by people who are convicted by the Holy Spirit to work for change in the church on this issue:

- Personally decide to stop using gender-exclusive words for people.
- Stop using masculine pronouns for God.
- In your personal prayer life, start calling God "Mother."
- Ask others to study this issue.
- Encourage pastors, worship committee, elders, deacons, or the leadership team to change worship language about persons.
- Pray. "This is a spiritual journey, a godly battle, and a righteous goal. Saturate all your longings, hopes, and actions with prayer" (Smith, 261-266).

Is Leadership for Roosters or Hens?

Not only does Sylvia hear people speaking of God in exclusively male terms. She also sees mostly men in church leadership positions. In the *Mennonite Brethren Herald,* a man pointed out that in the issue covering the Fresno '95 Conference of Mennonite Brethren Churches, the ratio of pictures of men to women was 40 to 6.

Why have over half the people of God been considered unfit for preaching, teaching, or overseeing a community of believers? Is that mandated by Scripture? Has it always been that way in the church? Is it only in this century that women are seeking to use their spiritual gifts of leadership in the church?

Actually, the answer to the last two questions is "No." There were women in positions of leadership in the early church. Women were ordained to various positions in the church even in the Middle Ages. A paper soon to be published by Harvard Divinity School cites a fifth-century papal letter that orders bishops to stop ordaining women as priests, and a ninth-century Italian bishop who stated that women shared the priestly ministry equally with men (Smith, 113).

Finding these women leaders, however, calls for some detective work. Often Bible translations and historical records have obscured the actual roles of women. Thus in Romans 16:1, Phoebe is called "a deacon" in many English versions, though the *Revised English Bible* has the courage to say "minister." When men are described, the same Greek word, *diakonos,* is often translated as "minister" or "servant" (see NRSV footnote; Rom. 15:8, Christ; 2 Cor. 3:6, Paul and others). Many readers fail to notice that Junia, a woman, was "prominent among the apostles" (Rom. 16:7).

A blatant example of altering historical records may be seen in the defacing of a mosaic in a Roman church, dating from about the fifth century. It depicts the head of a veiled woman with the title of episcopa (overseer, bishop) written over it. The woman's name Theodo[ra] was written vertically beside the figure. But the last two letters that make the name feminine had been removed from the mosaic and replaced by pieces from a later period, leaving the masculine name Theodo (Howe, 36-38).

Although there is scriptural and historical evidence for the leadership of women, women were gradually barred from leadership positions in the main church body. One reason was to guard against "heresy," since dissenting Christian groups sometimes allowed women leaders (as did the Montanists). In general, women received less education and were thought to be easily led astray (see 1 Tim. 2:14; 2 Tim. 3:6-7; Rev. 2:20). Unfair stereotyping was developing, and the male church hierarchy was closing ranks.

Another reason, in addition to pagan Greek influence, is that the Judaizers who caused Paul so much trouble brought back the idea of leader as priest (see chap. 2, above, on 1 Cor. 14:34-35). Women were barred from the priestly role on the basis that there were only male priests in the Old Testament and male disciples among the Twelve.

Related understandings reinterpreted Christian practices on the basis of the priestly role. The Lord's Supper became not the sharing of a fellowship meal symbolizing union with

Christ and other believers, but a sacrifice performed by the priest at an altar. Ordination was no longer the recognition of spiritual giftedness but a sacramental rite that imprinted a certain character on the priest, distinguishing him from all other Christians. Finally the understanding evolved that priestly service was valid no matter what the state of the priest's life or faith. The Roman church has maintained this concept of priesthood to this day.

Are these understandings of exclusively male leadership consistent with Anabaptist beliefs? There is much evidence that the sixteenth-century Anabaptist women took leadership positions, contrary to the male-dominated society in which they lived. They "held worship services, taught the Scriptures, distributed the sacraments, were elders and prophets, went on evangelistic tours, debated with theologians—and died for their faith" (Funk, 33; for examples, see Snyder and Hecht). In the records of *Martyrs Mirror,* women were about a third of those who testified to their faith and were martyred.

However, the Anabaptists lost this vision as they became "the quiet in the land" and adapted to cultures around them. Many of us came implicitly to accept a theology like a radio preacher's in this century. He declared that women had no right to preach because "God made roosters to crow and hens to lay eggs." In other words, men are the speakers, and women are the bearers of children (Bristow, 116). But Jesus clearly says that hearing and obeying the word of God is women's prime responsibility (Luke 10:39-42; 11:28; Mark 3:34-35).

In our time, Anabaptist churches and their members hold a range of beliefs and practices of women. Some include women in all forms of leadership and encourage suitable preparation for that. Others restrict them from ordination, yet allow them to serve as Sunday school teachers, conference representatives, and mission workers. Certainly the trend over the past decades has been a gradual opening of opportunities for women to use their gifts in the church.

And It Came to Pass . . .

This old phrase is used 452 times in the King James Version of the Bible, and it still holds a great deal of meaning for me. It means that at the right time, God's time, things will happen. All kinds of people will knowingly or unknowingly be conscripted to do the will of God, in "the fullness of time" (Gal. 4:4). No matter how hopeless it seems, eventually nothing can stand in God's way.

God's purposes may be deflected but never defeated. It also means that while we are called to live and witness to the values of the kingdom of God, the ultimate outcome is up to God. As the psalmist says, "If it had not been the Lord who was on our side, . . . the flood would have swept us away" (Ps. 124:2, 4). But when the Lord is on our side, or better yet, when we are on the Lord's side (Exod. 32:26; Josh. 24), the Lord will bring us through the waters.

When the entire message of Scripture is heard, there is no reason for women to have less responsibility than men for the life and leadership of the church. God has created women in the divine image, equal with men, and given men and women together the privilege of ruling the earth. God's covenant is offered to all who will obey the Lord.

Jesus calls both women and men to learn God's word and obey. Christ redeems women as well as men from the effects of the Fall. All believers are baptized into Christ. God's Spirit is lavishly poured out on young and old, men and women. Both women and men belong to the people of God chosen as a royal priesthood. Spiritual gifts have no gender designation in Scripture.

One day a friend of my seven-year-old grandson, Andy, complained that a video they were about to see was just for girls. "It is not," Andy replied. "Besides, girls are people, too." Sometimes "a little child shall lead" (Isa. 11:6). So don't be discouraged, all you little Sylvias and Andys, and grown-up

Sylvias and Andys. A lot has changed for women in my lifetime. Because God will bring it to pass, I'm sure the best is yet to come.

What Do You Think?

1. Why do we accept the "traditional" position on women from a later period rather than the earliest tradition of the Christian church?

2. Discuss attitudes and practices in your own congregation. Do both genders participate equally in all its ministries? How do you feel about it?

3. Has the issue of inclusive language ever been raised in your church? If yes, what was the response? If no, would you like it to be raised?

4. How do Anabaptist understandings of the Lord's Supper, the priesthood of all believers, and ordination open the way for women in leadership positions?

5. In the past, women were believed not to have the rational ability to serve as leaders. Now that this has been disproved, some are teaching that it is God's choice to put men in charge. Can this be supported biblically and theologically?

If You Want to Read More

Aldredge, Joan. *A Word for Girls and Boys*. Glad River Publications, 1993.

Bilezikian, Gilbert. *Beyond Sex Roles*. Baker Book House, 1985.

Bristow, John Temple. *What Paul Really Said About Women*. Harper & Row, 1988.

Ellul, Jacques. *The Subversion of Christianity*. Eerdmans, 1986.

Frank, Francine, and Frank Anshen. *Language and the Sexes*. State Univ. of N.Y. Press, 1983.

Funk, Herta, ed. *Study Guide on Women*. Faith & Life Press, 1975.

Hassey, Jeanette. *No Time for Silence*. Zondervan, 1986.

Howe, E. Margaret. *Women and Church Leadership.* Zondervan, 1982.

Hull, Gretchen G. *Equal to Serve.* Revell, 1987.

Malcolm, Kari Torjesen. *Women at the Crossroads.* InterVarsity Press, 1982.

Mennonite Encyclopedia, The. Articles on women. *ME*, 4:972-976; 5:933-935. Herald Press, 1959, 1990.

Metzger, Bruce M. "To the Reader." In *New Revised Standard Version Reference Bible.* Zondervan, 1990.

Smith, Paul R. *Is It OK to Call God Mother?* Hendrickson, 1993.

Snyder, C. Arnold, and Linda A. Huebert Hecht, eds. *Profiles of Anabaptist Women: Sixteenth Century Reforming Pioneers.* Wilfrid Laurier Univ. Press, 1996.

Swidler, Leonard. *Biblical Affirmations of Women.* Westminster, 1979.

Women's Concerns Report no. 114. " 'Hi, Preacher!'— Women in Pastoral Ministries." Mennonite Central Committee, May-June 1994.

261. 8343
P 4133

96622

LINCOLN CHRISTIAN COLLEGE AND SEMINARY

The Editor

CAROL PENNER, the editor of this book for the Mennonite Central Committee, lives in Vineland, Ontario, with her husband, Eugene. She spends most of her time caring for their two children, Katie and Alex. Their family is thankful to be a part of the community of First Mennonite Church in Vineland.

Penner works part-time for MCC Ontario doing education work in congregations on the subject of family violence. She has a doctoral thesis in progress on the subject of Mennonite peace theology.

3 4711 00087 3119